The South Pennines- Contents

Photographs: (BES) Pictures courtesy of Bradford Enterprise Service, (CBMC) City of Bradford Metropolitan Council, (KMC) Kirklees Metropolitan Council, (LCC) Leeds City Council, (MBC) Metropolitan Borough of Calderdale, (MH/LSWE) Malcolm Howarth/Last of the Summer Wine Exhibition, (NMP) National Museum of Photography, (YHTB) Yorkshire and Humberside Tourist Board, (YMM) Yorkshire Mining Museum.
Cover Photographs: Top - Ogden Reservoir (MBC); Middle left - Characters from the 'Last of the Summer Wine' television series (MH/LSWE); Bottom left - Brown Hill Reservoir (MBC); Middle right-Digley Reservoir (KMC); Bottom right - A view from the 'Emmerdale' television series (BES).

Discovery Guides Limited wish to thank all those persons, organisations, official bodies and their officers, for their kind assistance in the production of this publication.

WRITTEN BY: CHARLIE EMETT
ADDITIONAL WORK BY: JOHN BRIGHT & CAROLINE HILLERY
SERIES DESIGNER AND EDITOR: MALCOLM PARKER

PRINTED IN ENGLAND
PUBLISHED BY:
DISCOVERY GUIDES LIMITED
1 MARKET PLACE
MIDDLETON IN TEESDALE
COUNTY DURHAM DL12 0QG
TEL: (0833) 40638

ISBN 0-86309-088-5

TOURIST INFORMATION CENTRES

The following major information centres are open all the year round. Local information points may be opened in season.

BRADFORD
City Hall, Channing Way, Bradford,
West Yorkshire, BD1 1HY
Tel: Bradford (0274) 753678

BURNLEY
Burnley Mechanics, Manchester Road,
Burnley, Lancashire, BB11 1JA
Tel: Burnley (0282) 30055

HALIFAX
The Piece Hall, Westgate, Halifax,
West Yorkshire, HX1 1RE
Tel: Halifax (0422) 368725

HAWORTH
2 - 4 West Lane, Haworth, West Yorkshire,
B22 8EF
Tel: Keighley (0535) 642329

HEBDEN BRIDGE
1 Bridge Gate, Hebden Bridge,
West Yorkshire, HX7 8EX
Tel: Halifax (0422) 843831

HOLMFIRTH
49 - 51 Huddersfield Road, Holmfirth,
West Yorkshire, HD7 1JP
Tel: Huddersfield (0484) 684992

HUDDERSFIELD
3 Albion Street, Huddersfield,
West Yorkshire, HD1 2NW
Tel: Huddersfield (0484) 422133

ILKLEY
Station Road, Ilkley, West Yorkshire,
LS29 8HA
Tel: Ilkley (0943) 602319

NELSON
20 Scotland Road, Nelson, Lancashire,
BB9 7UU
Tel: Burnley (0282) 692890

OLDHAM
84 Union Street, Oldham, Gt. Manchester,
OL1 1DN
Tel: Manchester (061) 678 4654

RAWTENSTALL
41 - 45 Kay Street, Rawtenstall, Lancashire,
BB4 7LS
Tel: Rochdale (0706) 226590

ROCHDALE
The Clock Tower, Town Hall, Rochdale,
Lancashire, OL16 1AB
Tel: Rochdale (0706) 356592

SADDLEWORTH
Saddleworth Museum, High Street,
Uppermill, Gt. Manchester, OL3 6HS
Tel: Saddleworth (0457) 874093

SKIPTON
Victoria Square, Skipton, North Yorkshire,
BD23 1JF
Tel: Skipton (0756) 792809

TODMORDEN
15 Burnley Road, Todmorden, Lancashire,
OL14 7BU
Tel: Rochdale (0706) 818181

OTHER USEFUL ADDRESSES

THE BRONTË SOCIETY
Brontë Parsonage, Haworth, near Keighley,
West Yorkshire, BD22 8DR
Tel: Keighley (0535) 642323

GREATER MANCHESTER PASSENGER TRANSPORT EXECUTIVE
PO Box 429, 9 Portland Street, Piccadilly
Gardens, Manchester, M60 1HX
Tel: Manchester (061) 228 6400 / 7811

KEIGHLEY AND WORTH VALLEY RAILWAY SOCIETY
Haworth Station, Keighley, West Yorkshire,
BD22 8NJ
Tel: Keighley (0535) 643629 (talking timetable), 645214 (general)

LANCASHIRE COUNTY COUNCIL, PUBLIC TRANSPORT ENQUIRIES
Winckley House, PO Box 9, Cross Street,
Preston, PR1 8RD
Tel: Preston (0772) 264563 / 263333

S.C.O.S.P.A. (STANDING CONFERENCE OF SOUTH PENNINES AUTHORITIES)
Jacob's Well, Manchester Road, Bradford,
BD1 5RN

WEATHER CALL (recorded information)
Lancashire, Tel 0898 500 416
Yorkshire, Tel 0898 500 417

WEST YORKSHIRE PASSENGER TRANSPORT EXECUTIVE
Wellington House, 40 - 50 Wellington Street,
Leeds, LS1 2DE
Tel: (0532) 440988 and (0924) 375555

Introduction to the South Pennines

There are **four distinct areas** in the South Pennines: the Uplands, once the home of prehistoric man and now a source of peat, stone and coal; the valleys which are increasingly being flooded to supply towns with water; the hillside terraces; and the cloughs.

The terraces, which were farmed during the Middle Ages have been developed into villages. The origins of the textile industry are there - the cloughs or narrow sided valleys were ideal locations for water powered mills. The main valleys became the final home of the textile industry.

The grazing of **sheep** has always been the mainstay of farming in the South Pennines although until recently few of those who produced the meat could afford to eat it. The staple grain was oats, until cheap corn from elsewhere became readily available in the C19th.

Prior to the Industrial Revolution, communications consisted of long distance paths and pack horse routes. The poor soil encouraged farmers to diversify and the **manufacture of cloth** provided just the opportunity. People began to settle in weaving communities, turnpike roads were developed and cloth halls were built for trading. During the latter half of the C18th and the first half of the C19th tremendous expansion took place, reflecting the growth of the British Empire. **Mills and factories** replaced cottage industry, firstly with the help of water power, then with steam. Canals were built and coal was brought along them to the area. As the population increased, more land was enclosed to contain dairy herds.

Living conditions for the workers were so harsh and squalid that their need for improvement could not be ignored. Building societies were formed in Halifax and other places as a form of self help. Some mill owners, like 'Honest John' Fielder of Todmorden, cared for their workers and urged reforms in working conditions. Civic pride was expressed in fine public buildings. A reduction in factory hours allowed some time for recreation and people exercised their freedom to roam the hills.

Today, the textile industry has declined, nature has reclaimed old industrial land and the **footpaths** have become a major tourist asset. The South Pennines and freedom of access to them for everybody have become highly emotive symbols for the rambling community of England, for these hills and high places that form the backbone of the country have helped countless millions of people living and working in the industrial towns of the North to endure the dark days of the Industrial Revolution. It was to the high moors that they came, seeking a taste of freedom, while the more intimate wooded valleys allowed a closer contact with nature.

The best way to discover the South Pennines is on foot. There you will find some **outstandingly beautiful scenery....** and all within reach of the earthy plains of Lancashire and Yorkshire. So take to the moors and the valleys, savour them and there you will discover fine views, a natural peace and fresh air by the lungful. Even our industrial heritage adds interest to many of the walks, and the tow paths of three trans-Pennine canals provide easy strolling for the not so energetic.

Nowhere in Great Britain is the story of the Great British woollen and cotton industries, from the mediaeval cottage to the development of the mill, better illustrated than in the South Pennines. Tucked into the hillsides are **historic villages** full of weavers' cottages, easily recognised by their long rows of stone mullioned windows. In the **small towns** that nestle alongside fast flowing rivers, picturesque groups of stone cottages, 'ginnels' and courtyards intermix with magnificent mills set proudly amidst heather clad hills.

Within a few miles of this absorbing countryside there is a range of museums, art galleries, mill shops, markets and shopping centres ever ready to cheer the wet weather blues.

There are more **places to visit** around the South Pennines than anywhere else of comparable size outside London...... and with enough variety to suit all tastes and age groups. After all, it is the combination of family fun and entertainment together with picnics in idyllic surroundings, fine country walks, good food and ale and true South Pennines hospitality that will make your stay there memorable.

At the day's end, when your legs begin to tire and the sun sinks in the west, the South Pennines will offer you the finest restaurants, traditional pubs, superb concert halls or just a comfortable bed. The choice is yours.

Celebrations are fun and when there is something extra special to celebrate, merriment becomes unbounded and cheers the hearts of benefactor and beneficiary alike; eyes sparkle, smiles become broader, laughter and conviviality bubble near the surface and are frequently on show.

This special celebration comes to you thanks to the hard work and dedication of a very special organisation, the **Standing Conference of South Pennine Authorities** (SCOSPA) which was formed in 1974 to give a unified approach to informal recreation provision, wildlife and heritage conservation and its interpretation in the South Pennines, and to promote the sensitive development of tourism so that it conserves and improves the best features in the region.

On it are Bradford, Burnley, Calderdale, Craven, Kirklees, Lancashire County Council, Pendle, Rochdale and Rossendale, together with organisations representing the voluntary sector. The members of SCOSPA believe that a measure of voluntary co-operation and a strong will to make well-defined intention a reality is by far the best way to bring people together, even across the great Pennine divide.

Tourists in the past have either tended to ignore - or deliberately avoid - the South Pennines, or to concentrate their blinkered attention upon one 'honeypot' attraction. It was surmised that the close proximity of so many large manufacturing centres, with their smoke and grime, must inevitably minimise the potential beauty of the upland regions, for who on holiday wants to be always in sight of industrial squalor? The braver traveller, or the more ardent Brontë fan, dashed into Haworth, soaked it up, and dashed out again - it may be thought that many still do.

Times are changing though. There has grown a greater realisation that there is indeed real beauty and solitude and large open spaces to be found on the South Pennine hills; that the towns themselves are cleaning up and revealing unexpected attractiveness; that the quality of cultural and social life in the region is the equal of that found anywhere. Furthermore a new appreciation of our **industrial heritage** has altered people's perceptions too, and features once avoided are now sought out with interest.

In addition, the area has undoubtedly had its **image** changed in the view of millions of people through its exposure on television. The popular '**Last of the Summer Wine**' has created a fame for Holmfirth, where the series is centred, which has probably overtaken that of the Haworth Parsonage, home of the Brontë sisters and object of pilgrimage by students for more than a hundred years.

'**Emmerdale**' too, filmed around Esholt and Leathley, has done its part in showing the rest of the country that the north does not in fact consist solely of pitheaps, railway yards, out dated factories and rural slums, as was commonly thought, and the devotees flock in.

The celebration of an area like the South Pennines can be seen as a celebration of **opposites**, a celebration of hill and dale, of man-made and natural, past and present - and gloriously, east and west - Yorkshire and Lancashire, the red rose and the white, at last (here, if not in early history or on the sportsfield!) in harmony.

The beauties and attractions of the region may only just be coming to the notice of the outside world, but they have long been treasured by the people who live amongst them. It is inevitable that the notion of the hitherto secret places of the South Pennines being over-run by tourists will not have universal appeal, and the opening up of the area to outsiders has to be done with **care and sensitivity,** to safeguard the interests of the local people as well as those invited in, and it is for this task that SCOSPA is particularly important.

The South Pennine region can, perhaps, be best seen in all its diversity by splitting it into **four easily recognisable areas,** each with its own individual character: from the broad valley of Airedale in the north to the 'Pennine Edge' and Rossendale, the southern gateway to the region; from Pendle and the Lancashire Calder in the west to the deep valleys of Pennine Yorkshire in the east.

AIREDALE - SKIPTON AND THE BRONTË COUNTRY The Aire, flowing from its source north of Malham Cove, forms the natural northern boundary to the South Pennines. The broad valley is shared by **Craven and Bradford** Districts and is guarded at its western end by the historic market town of **Skipton.**

Take a boat trip from Skipton along the Leeds-Liverpool Canal where the Five Rise Locks at Bingley present a marvellous sight. Although pleasure cruising along the canal is becoming increasingly popular, it is also plied by commercial firms like Apollo Canal Carriers Ltd. (See 'Outdoor and Leisure Activities').

Ilkley Moor is to the north of the Aire Valley with Haworth Moor and its famous Brontë village to the south. Secluded Lothersdale with its lush pastures is near Skipton. From Keighley, the Keighley and Worth Valley Railway will take you to Haworth and Oxenhope; and from either place you can join the Worth Way and explore on foot this engaging landscape of pasture, gritstone walls, hill villages and reservoirs.

Airedale is well off for country railways, like the Embsay Steam Railway near Skipton, preserved in steam.

CALDER, COLNE AND HOLME - PENNINE YORKSHIRE (BALDERDALE AND KIRKLEES) These **three valleys** which, with their many feeders, cut deeply into the Pennine uplands, give spectacular views from their moortop heads where old pack horse routes and other roads descend precipitously into small towns like Todmorden, Marsden, Hebden Bridge, Ripponden and Holmfirth.

On the '**slacks**' above the steep sided, wooded valleys are miles of gritstone walls, punctuated by clog-worn stiles and ancient pathways linking weaving settlements.

The National Trust is custodian of two outstanding sites of nature conservation interest, Hardcastle Crags near **Hebden Bridge** and **Marsden Moor** between the Colne Valley and Saddleworth.

The Pennine Way cuts across moorland roads before descending into Lothersdale on its way northwards to the Yorkshire Dales. By walking sections of the Calderdale Way, Kirklees Way or the full 12 miles (19 kms) length of the Colne Valley Circular, you will see the best of Pennine Yorkshire. There are walking and heritage trails galore like Wesley, Luddites and Colners, and these are both exciting and informative - and great fun.

ROSSENDALE AND ROCHDALE (THE PENNINE EDGE) The massive **gritstone blocks** of Blackstone Edge **tower** above Littleborough and Rochdale, which shares **Healey Dell Local Nature Reserve**, a countryside gem, with Rossendale District. Views over the edge are dominated by **Hollingworth Lake**, with its popular Country Park and Visitor Centre, the starting point for a number of interesting self-guided trails.

The recently opened Summit Circuit Trail, a little lower down, offers similar panoramic views over the same vista and interprets it by means of a prize-winning 'Groundwork' leaflet. Rochdale and Rossendale are both hosts to separate 'Groundwork Trusts', urban fringe projects which promote **environmental improvements** and access initiatives through developing partnerships with the local communities.

Piethorne, Watergrove and Cowan reservoirs all offer informal recreational opportunities that will blow away the cobwebs.

To the west of Rochdale, the well wooded Ashworth and Cheesden Valleys are a treasure trove of **water powered industrial heritage.** The deeply incised 'valley' between Rawtenstall and Bacup, along with the Whitworth area, invites locals and visitors to discover Rossendale, use the Heritage Trails and enjoy the area.

LANCASHIRE'S CALDER AND PENDLE COUNTRY (BURNLEY AND PENDLE DISTRICTS) The **broad North East Lancashire valley** is bounded by the Pennine Watershed of Black Hameldon/Boulsworth Hill to the east and Pendle Hill to the west.

The last glaciation filled the valley with ice which extended half-way up the Pennine ridge, creating interesting overflow channels for the meltwater. By far the **largest and most dramatic** of these is the Oliviger Gorge, enclosed to the south by the cliffs of Thievely Scout. To the north of the gorge, Worsthorne has a variety of walking routes to explore, whilst the Barley area, with its inviting picnic site is the base for climbing Pendle's 'big end'. Nestling at the foot of Boulsworth Hill, **Wycoller Country Park** is an old weaving hamlet in an idyllic valley setting and strictly shuns any trappings of the C20th, to the delight of visitors. Passing close by is the route of the Pendle Way which, together with its associated short circular walks, gives no excuse for not venturing into the countryside.

So join in the celebrations and have a 'reet good Pennine time': South Pennine, that is.

A Short History of the Area

About **10,000 years ago,** at the end of the last Ice Age, the first humans entered Yorkshire in the wake of the shrinking ice cap, which had previously covered Northern England. At that time the appearance of the land was very different from what we see today. There was a land connection with Europe across the southern half of the North Sea, making it possible for groups of Stone Age hunters to cross from North Germany and Jutland to Eastern England in search of food and shelter. They were omnivorous and often sheltered in caves like Victoria Cave above Settle. When these first people came the climate was sub-Arctic and the animals these Old Stone Age or Palaeolithic people hunted were mammoth, woolly rhinoceros and reindeer.

During the **5,000 years following** the arrival of these forest migrants the climate steadily improved and a richer natural vegetation began to cover the land.

Around **3,000 BC Neolithic** or New Stone Age settlers arrived from the continent, by which time the North Sea and the English Channel had more or less assumed their present shape. This means that these people must have arrived in boats, probably dug-out canoes.

Neolithic man learned arable farming and the domestication of animals. He could make pottery, weave cloth and make baskets, and his achievement meant that it was no longer necessary to live a semi-nomadic life. Neolithic people buried their dead with some ceremony in chambered mounds called barrows.

Bronze was introduced circa 1800 BC by the arrival of the **Beaker people**. They were eventually conquered by Celtic speaking invaders who had entered Gaul from the Mediterranean and who settled in Britain to become the Ancient Britons or in the north, the Brigantes. They resisted the Roman invaders in the early years of the Christian era. The Brigantes knew how to make iron and were skilled horsemen.

The Roman invasion of the North of England began around 73 AD and lasted until early in the C5th. At that time the topography was very different from that of today. The Vale of York was marshy and impassable in many places. There were a lot of thickly forested areas, of which little remains today except in place names on maps like the Forest of Elmet, near Leeds.

Simultaneously with the arrival of the first humans in Yorkshire, the first human settlers in **Lancashire** migrated northwards across the peat mosses of the Mersey Valley. They kept to the Pennine uplands where the oak and the birch forests were thinner, because this made hunting easier than in the deeper, wetter forests of the plain.

When Neolithic man had arrived along the western foothills of the Pennines he had brought **arable farming** with him, sowing seeds, cutting grass with stone sickles and keeping herds of cattle, sheep and goats. He had begun to clear the upland forests and, although he had made a start on building dwellings of mud or wood, he continued to inhabit the moorland caves his predecessors had occupied. Neolithic burial chambers have been found on Anglezarke Moor.

The **Bronze Age** coincided with a period of drier weather in the North West, so substantial and waterproof dwellings became less essential. This change in the weather pattern may explain the scarcity of known sites for this period.

The **Iron Age** brought much wetter weather, and remains of this period are more substantial.

Around 80 AD **the Romans** built a fortified road, linking Chester and York, eastwards from Manchester, then a timbered auxiliary fort named '**Mamucium**'. There, there was a fork, one road being routed via Castleshaw and Slack, the other taking a more northerly route, climbing over Blackstone Edge to Littleborough and crossing the moors to Ilkley.

In the countryside the **patterns of farming** established in the Iron Age continued virtually unchanged. The cattle and horse breeders of the western Pennines still lived in stone huts with walled enclosures nearby for their livestock. Beyond collecting taxes in the form of hides, the Romans did not interfere with the hill farmers lives.

The eastern Pennines remained largely unoccupied throughout the Roman occupation.

In the mid-C6th warlike **Teutonic tribes** crossed the North Sea from Friesland, Jutland and Saxony. They had for many years raided east Yorkshire, but began to establish permanent settlements in the Wolds. From these footholds, these Angles soon spread westwards to York and Ripon and along the valley lands of the River Ouse. Some settled along the Northumbrian coast. Others reached the Millstone Grit area of the South Pennines, cleared places in the woodlands and named them in their dialect with a suffix 'leah'. This is now recognised in **places names** as 'ley'. Ilkley is a good example. The woodlands were thickest on the gritstone soils and the distribution of place names ending in 'ley' shows a close link with such soil areas.

Christianity, which Roman-Celtic missionaries had brought to the Angles before the Romans were recalled, was seriously disrupted during the C9th by Scandinavian invaders, called **Vikings** after 'Vik' the creek or inlet from which they had set sail in their long boats.

York apart, the **Vikings** usually **avoided the Roman towns** and fortresses, most of which were in decay anyway. They used parts of the Roman roads but also developed their own system of tracks to suit their different needs as farmers and traders.

The tracks made by the Anglo Saxons often tended to be cross or star shaped, radiating from a valley settlement. One road ran down to the river with its richer meadows, another went uphill, through the common pasture to unreclaimed woodland. The others went more or less horizontally along the valley, through open arable fields and wasteland to link up with similar tracks stretching outwards from the neighbours on either side. This explains why to this day many of the **by-ways in the South Pennines** zigzag through the countryside in a series of right angle bends.

Comparatively few people lived in the South Pennines in **mediaeval times** and those who did had very primitive living standards. They lived in self-made mud hovels made from pairs of timbers lashed together at the top, anchored in the ground by low, wood framed walls and roofed with turf or thatch. It was difficult to stand upright in them and often the ground was hollowed out to give extra height. The earth floor was covered with rushes, straw or furze and cleaned out whenever fresh material was available. Dogs, hens, pigs and cattle shared the accommodation with members of the family and in so doing provided heat to supplement that from the smoky fire in the middle of the floor. Food cooked over this fire was mainly porridge and vegetable soups. Most households had no facilities for making oatmeal bread or brewing ale and these were got in from outside. Ewes and cows were both milked and cheese was an important variant in the diet. Fresh meat was a treat for most families in autumn, when most of the cattle were slaughtered. If the cost of salt from Cheshire could be afforded, some meat was preserved in tubs of brine for consumption throughout winter. Wool was used for clothes and hempen cloth was a popular substitute for linen. **Life was far from comfortable** and the impact of cattle sickness, harvest failures and the plague, especially the Black Death in 1348-1349, made living in the Southern Pennines, and almost anywhere else, nearly impossible.

The South Pennines played no significant part in the dynastic quarrel for the throne of England between the houses of Lancaster and York. In fact the **Wars of the Roses** hardly touched the area and no battle was fought there.

The **Dissolution of the Monasteries** by Henry VIII did not please everyone. There was the threat of a rising in Yorkshire, which was thought to be staunch Roman Catholic. Unrest grew with the suppression of the smaller monasteries in 1536 and a rising which began in Lincolnshire soon spread across Yorkshire where Robert Aske, a lawyer, was persuaded to lead the rebels in what became known as the Pilgrimage of Grace. One of the towns that gave him whole hearted support was **Halifax.** The uprising failed and Aske was hanged at York.

When Elizabeth became Queen she chose an **ecclesiastical policy** which was mid-way between Protestantism and Roman Catholicism, which proved to be unpopular. The Pope excommunicated her and devout Catholics found their loyalties divided between Pope and Crown. From 1580, **Jesuits and secular priests** trained in Rome began missionary activities in Lancashire, hoping to regain lost ground. The most famous of these Jesuits was Edmund Campion. While he was strengthening Roman Catholicism, the reformed religion began to make progress through south-east Lancashire, which included South Pennine villages that were supplying Manchester with cloth. **Puritanism spread** out from Manchester, as literature and ideas were carried to South Pennine centres of population along established trade routes.

While Roman Catholic priests and Puritan teachers campaigned to bring their versions of the Gospel to the people, popular religion remained a mixture of **magic and superstition**. Most villages had charmers, wise men and women who were thought to have special powers of divination and prediction and who could command life, death and disease. Their remedies were charms or herbal potions. Their powers of wizardry were regarded as gifts and as being hereditary. It was believed that such powers could be used for good or evil. Puritan teachers became very active in condemning this witchcraft and magic. They saw it as a battle between spiritual Christ and Anti-Christ in the same way that the natural world was divided between Protestants and Roman Catholics.

It was not sufficient for witches to be condemned as magicians or charmers. They had to be identified as agents and instruments of the Devil. Elizabeth Southerns or 'Old Demdike' as she was generally known, was the head of a family of **witches in Pendle** and was described by Thomas Potts, clerk to the judge at her trial as 'a very old woman, about the age of four score years and had been a witch for fifty years' She was branded as 'a general agent for the Devil in all these parts'.

It was two entirely different kinds of magic that were later to radically alter the face of the South Pennines: **cotton** on the western side and **wool** to the east.

If a cotton thread had snapped on the western side of the South Pennines as it did on the eastern slopes, that part of South Lancashire would have developed differently, But the climate turned out to be ideally suited for the **spinning and weaving** of cotton. The Pennines cooled the prevailing westerlies and condensed the vapours which gave the air just the humidity needed for spinning the cotton thread. Thanks to the Millstone Grit there was abundant water, coal was on the door-step and, not far away, lay Liverpool, shipping outlet to the world.

The **manufacture of cotton** in the South Pennines began in the C16th. It was used in conjunction with linen in making fabrics, the warp being supplied by the linen with the cotton supplying only the weft. The name of this mixed material was Fustian.

Cotton manufacture was a classic example of **early capitalistic industry** in which the capitalist owned the material used, passed it to the workers for processing in their homes and marketed the product. It was a system that lasted well into the C18th because those remarkable inventions like Hargreave's Spinning Jenny, while enabling workers to increase their output did not require them to be concentrated at factories. It was not until about 1770, when machinery was driven by horses, water power and eventually steam, that factory production was necessary. From then on **cotton spinning mills** spread rapidly.

By that time Arkwright's improvements to spinning machinery had enabled yarn to be spun suitable for warps as well as wefts. **Weaving** was still carried out in homes; the first power looms took years to perfect and weaving did not quite cease to be a home occupation until the middle of the C19th.

For many years Great Britain was by far the **world's largest exporter of cotton goods.** Between 1880 and the First World War about two thirds of the world's imports of cotton manufacturers were supplied by Lancashire, a large percentage of that coming from mills in the South Pennines. Exports peaked during the four year period from 1910 to 1913. Then began a steady decline, until by the late 1950s the value of exported cotton yarns and fabrics together amounted to less than four percent of Britain's export of manufactured goods.

Simultaneously with the growth of the cotton industry on the western side of the South Pennines, the **woollen industry** was undergoing a similar but more painful transformation on its eastern side.

Although **the Industrial Revolution** in the South Pennines began in the late C18th, the rural landscape prior to its arrival remained substantially the same for the next hundred years, although some villages and towns changed out of all recognition within the lifetimes of many of their inhabitants. The Industrial Revolution affected everybody because of the enormity of the **upheavals** dictated by it. For the term not only describes a process of industrialisation; it also includes the resulting changes in social and political relationships between people.

The changes in **working conditions** and the impact of new inventions on traditional forms of employment led to opposition from traditional craft workers. Along the eastern side of the South Pennines the work of skilled croppers, or shearmen, was replaced by the shearing frame and the gig mill, which would produce the same output from one eighth of the labour employed using traditional methods of working the cloth. Machine breakers or '**Luddites**' attempted to halt the introduction of gig mills in Leeds in 1791, but with little success. By 1817 there were 72 gig mills in Yorkshire and a third of the shearmen were unemployed.

Power looms began to replace the work of the handloom weavers. In **Bingley,** near Bradford, when an attempt was made to bring in new machinery, workers tried to smash it. There were **Luddite riots** in mills at Huddersfield and Leeds. The most serious incident was the murder of William Horsfall, of Ottiwells, near Huddersfield, who had boasted of his hatred of Luddites. Horsfall loaded a cannon and armed his men to fend off an attack on his mill. The leaders of the assault, in which Horsfall was **murdered,** were all found guilty. Seventeen were **hanged,** one was transported for life and six were transported for seven years.

When steam-driven power looms were introduced in the 1820s the livelihood of handloom weavers was even more severely affected. In 1826 **the Riot Act** was read in Bradford, when 250 protesters marched on a worsted mill. Two of the attackers were killed and several injured when shots were fired. However, such demonstrations brought only a temporary halt to the introduction of new machinery. Nine years after the riots, the Huddersfield mills had 378 power looms in operation.

The rapid growth of industry along both sides of the South Pennines and elsewhere resulted in **social conditions** which shocked many people and led to Government enquiries and Acts of Parliament.

In 1844 Fredrick Engels described **Bradford** like this: '....within reigns the same filth and discomfort as Leeds. The older portions of the town are built upon steep hillsides and are narrow and irregular. In the lanes, alleys and courts lie **filth and debris** in heaps; the houses are ruinous, dirty and miserable.... In general, the portions of the valley bottom in which working men's cottages have crowded between the tall factories, are amongst the worst built and dirtiest districts of the whole town. In the newer portions of this, as of every other factory town, the cottages are more regular, being built in rows, but they share here too, all **the evils** incident to the customary method of providing working men's dwellings.... the same is true of the remaining towns of the West Riding, especially **Barnsley, Halifax and Huddersfield.**'

The Industrial Revolution created great wealth in the towns of the South Pennines. This was seen partly in the **vast increase of population** in part with the rapid growth of every type of industry. But in terms of income there was a great inequality, the differing lifestyles of factory owners, managers and their employees being poles apart.

This contrast between the indolent rich employer and his forgotten starving employee is frequently pointed out, but often the **first generation manufacturers** themselves worked very long hours indeed and took great financial risks. Despite low taxation levels many failed and sank back to, or below, the level from which they had come. Many of those who did succeed encouraged their children in charitable and political work to improve the lot of the poor. They did not change the system which had made their money; but this is not surprising.

The lives of many mill owners were not as luxurious or irresponsible as is frequently suggested. Despite their wealth, their **homes,** though better than those of their employees, were small and unimpressive when compared with the homes of landed gentry.

Before the First World War the South Pennines had gloried in the strength of its two major industries, cotton and wool. During the conflict, cotton suffered from a **shortage of man-power** and a reduction in shipping space and, with peace, the underlying problems of the cotton and wool industries were exposed. **Loss of export markets** in textiles continued as India, Britain's largest pre-war market, became virtually self-sufficient, and competitors like Italy and Japan proved more efficient with newer machines, lower wages and better industrial organisation.

Adjusting to post war conditions was difficult. **Unemployment** was widespread and there were wage cuts: 1929 heralded the Wall Street Crash and a world slump.

Perhaps the worst result of unemployment was demoralisation: the hanging about on street corners; the dreary succession of empty days without hope. **Public library** reading rooms became popular, partly because free daily papers were available and partly because there were few clubs for the unemployed. Evening classes flourished and billiard halls and **cinemas** were filled to capacity. For a few pence you could enter a magic world far removed from shoddy reality and, for a few hours each week, escape into a celluloid world of fantasy. Here business was brisk; a change of programme every Thursday and two main features each week. Amateur **sports** clubs also flourished and attendances at rugby league and cricket matches increased.

The Second World War put an end to unemployment and provided **a sense of purpose** which was easily grasped by those who had felt life to be aimless in the depression. Churchill encapsulated this proud, new spirit in his rallying speeches.

The post war years have seen **dramatic change,** much for the better. Town centres have been pulled apart and rebuilt in a pollution free atmosphere. **New industries** have replaced the old, staple ones. Much has been done; much remains to do. It is an on-going process, but today the spirit and the will to do it is strong.

The fringes of the South Pennines are highly urbanised and a legacy of obsolete buildings remains along with other unwanted bequests of the Industrial Revolution. **Clean Air Acts** have greatly improved the physical environment and the change from coal to gas, electricity and oil has worked wonders. The Government has made money available for the **reclamation of land** and the cleaning of churches and public buildings. Conservation has come into its own and everybody has benefited.

If, today, there is barely a metre of space along the edge of the South Pennines, there is enough and to spare on the moors, where you can ride or walk for miles in **splendid solitude**. It is a land of reservoirs, for these **broad, lonely heights** supply the surrounding plains of West Yorkshire, Lancashire and Cheshire with water; so the practicality remains.

The hills with their rivers and reservoirs have, however, not always been entirely benevolent. In 1977 a tremendous thunderstorm created a flood in Holmfirth in which three lives were lost; and for almost a century it was known as **the Great Flood.** An arrow carved into the stone of Wagstaff's Boot and Shoe shop in Station Road marks the height it reached.

Then in 1852, following a series of heavy rains, Bilberry Reservoir burst its banks with 450 million litres (100 million gallons) of water cascading down the Holm Valley and reaching unprecedented heights in Holmfirth. A plaque on the column in Towngate clearly shows the level reached by the water. The flood was a **tragedy of unbelievable proportions** in which 81 lives were lost. Holmbridge, directly under the reservoir was badly affected, the waters rising to 1½ metres (5 feet) within the church. In Hinchliffe Moss six three-storey houses were swept away in Water Street alone and 42 people perished. Along the valley, mills, farms, cottages and animals were swept away.

The next great flood occurred on **Whit Monday, 1944,** after a cloudburst which swelled the River Holme in places to a height of some 6 metres (almost 20 feet). Three people drowned and 200 houses in Holmfirth were flooded. The height reached by this flood is recorded on a plaque on the left hand side of the door of the Elephant and Castle.

In the South Pennines in social terms the **quality of life** is good. Music and theatre have participated in the national revival and sport, both amateur and professional, is enjoying an often boisterous following. Despite increased mobility of population, the traditional gregarious spirit, as measured in the number of pubs, clubs and churches, is as real as ever. The high circulation of local newspapers emphasises the **close identification** of many people with both the local and regional community. In spite of modern scepticism, civic pride and confidence in the future is strong.

The Industrial Revolution left the South Pennines with money problems but it also fostered a local pride, a distinctive character and a sense of humour which the C20th cannot destroy and these are the very features which make it such an enjoyable and rewarding place to visit.

The following is but a selection from an area rich in ghostly stories:

BRADFORD

'Fred', who haunts the Wyke Non-Political Club, first made his presence felt in 1972. Shortly before midnight, a member of staff decided to visit the ladies'-room. As she opened the door she saw, standing close to her, a **bedraggled grey haired man** with staring eyes. On turning to run from the room, she felt a cold hand under hers on the door handle. It was minus a thumb. Terrified, the lady fainted.

At the same club, unaccountably, a table and four chairs were found on the stage, and four wet rings were on the table, with no glasses nearby. At another time, a cleaner was returning to the main hall when she almost stumbled over **the spectral figure of a man** sitting on some steps, holding his head in his hands.

The building lights have turned themselves on and off and there is a feeling that someone is watching. 'Fred', it would seem, is a very active ghost, yet no one knows who he is. The club is built on the site of a dye house and a mill dam. Many years ago a millwright who had lost a thumb of one hand was **accidentally drowned** in the dam, though why he would want to frighten the club's staff remains a mystery.

BURNLEY

The ghost of **Lady O'Hagen**, the last resident of Towneley Hall, is said to drive along Manchester Road in her pony and trap, always stopping outside one of the houses she frequently visited in the latter years of her life.

HALIFAX

The ghost of comedian and playwright Clarence 'Tubby' Turner is reputed **to haunt the Palace Theatre.** It was on the stage there that he collapsed and died in the early 1950s whilst performing his famous deckchair sketch. An unconfirmed story relates that when an amateur dramatic society was presenting a Turner play 'Summat For Nowt', one of the lady performers who had difficulties with her lines, spotted a man, unknown to her standing in the wings, mouthing the words to her. She later learned that her description fitted that of Turner.

HAWORTH PARSONAGE

Emily Brontë has been seen on various occasions walking 'with her head bowed deep in thought' along the narrow path leading from her home to Top Withens, the location used for the Heathcliffe residence. There is no set pattern to her visits; **the phantom** has been seen in the evenings and early afternoons, but mostly during the latter half of the year.

HEBDEN BRIDGE

A Hebden Bridge couple who shared their home with a well-loved **black and white cat** called Thomas, were upset by his sudden demise. Thomas was gently wrapped in a cloth and buried under a small tree where for hours during the summer he had earlier sat or slept. It was snowing quite hard during the burial.

A couple of evenings after the cat's death, the lady was alone in the house when she heard **the latch rattle** on the door just as Thomas had used to rattle it from the window ledge. She told her husband about it when he returned home later but he didn't believe her, nor did he a few nights later when it happened again.

The following evening, however, her husband saw the latch move, dashed to the door and opened it; but there was no one there. There was, however, the **single imprint** of a cat's paw in the fresh snow.

KEIGHLEY

East Riddlesden Hall, a C17th manor house near the A560 at Keighley, and once owned by the Rishworth family is haunted by **an unidentified lady.** Wearing a long blue dress, she swishes aimlessly along corridors and in and out of rooms in which several people have seen **a cradle rocking** without being touched by human hands. Perhaps the rocker was the lady in blue.

RIPPONDEN

On the ancient pack horse road across Blackstone Edge at Soyland, near Ripponden, there stands an isolated C18th inn with some C19th additions. At one period during the C18th, when it was called The Blue Ball Inn, the landlord, Iron Will, who was known as a lecher, raped **a sewing wench** called Faith and then drowned her on the moor. On quiet winter nights **her spirit** can be heard running across the floor of what is thought to have been Iron Will's bedroom, presumably attempting to escape his unwelcome amorous advances.

From Neolithic times, simple country folk had never ceased to venerate the **Horned God**. During the centuries of Roman rule and for many generations afterwards he had been worshipped openly with music, dancing and processions in which the young girls scattered flowers before him on feast days. The church pandered to these jollifications, calling him **Jack-in-the-Green** or **Robin Goodfellow**. But gradually the rule of the church grew firmer, less and less licence was permitted and, eventually, the Old God's high days were taken over by the Christian saints.

Yet the Old God did not die, because people had need of him. They found no satisfaction in a religion that failed to provide an occasional outlet for their love of revelry. Many of them had more faith in t**he bawdy goat-man**, a provider of good harvests and bonnie babies, than in a sad figure hanging from the Cross who, anyway, appeared powerless against the plague.

So for many centuries the weekly esbat and **the monthly sabbat** became a regular feature of country life throughout Western Europe and for centuries there was nothing particularly wicked about them. These were usually held at the time of a full moon and four times a year **grand sabbats** were held at which several congregations gathered together to celebrate the Old God's feasts. These were 2nd February (Candlemas), April 30th (Walpurgisnacht), 1st August (Lammas) and 31st October (Hallowe'en).

The simple folk who, for the rest of the week could afford only the poorest fare, pooled ali the good things they had brought - poultry, poached game, fruit, cakes, honey and home-brewed drinks - and had a real tuck in. **The feast** over and filled with strong ale and cowslip and dandelion wine, the fun became fast and furious. **Adultery** was held to be a sin by the Christian God but the Old Religion taught that this aided fertility in crops and cattle.

With **the coming of the Reformation** in the C16th the sabbats began to take on a different character, largely because many venal but tolerant priests were swept away or forced to become zealots. A new type of clergy was born; vociferous, puritanical men who were determined to **enforce conformity** on everyone. These were the ones who stigmatised the Old God as the Devil and threatened any parishioner who attended a sabbat with eternal torment in the fires of Hell. This scared many good folk into foregoing further visits to sabbats. These puritans preached with conviction about the goodness of Christ; and did so in English, which everyone could understand.

Outside the Church only **the worst elements** of the people were left to the Old God. They were, for the most part, outlaws and robbers who lived in the woods, men and women who were by nature, anarchists. They were greedy and unscrupulous people, prepared to risk discovery and punishment by the Church in order to obtain the secrets of casting spells, making love philtres and poisons to be sold secretly for good money. In this way the midnight picnics and the bawdy gaiety became **blasphemous parodies** of the Christian faith.

Henceforth anyone wanting to attend one had to be **initiated into a coven**, which was run by terror. The initiate had to deny Christ, spit on the Cross and perform other obscene acts, including the signing of a pact with the Devil in his or her own blood.

The Pendle witches, of whom the most notorious was Elizabeth Southern, or **Old Demdike** as she was generally known, are familiar to many through Harrison Ainsworth's famous novel. Not only was Old Demdike a witch, she brought up her children to be witches and instructed her grand-children in witchcraft. This was not unusual. The handing down in families of the secret art was common practice.

To enable **a good feast at sabbats**, the Pendle witches simply went to the house of a well-to-do farmer and helped themselves to what they fancied from the pantry. This custom was also practised in many other areas and the covens were so feared that no farmer protested.

Some of the cottage chimneys in Lothersdale have flat slabs protruding from their sides. These were so placed so that **witches flying past** to or from Pendle could rest en route and refresh themselves with food thoughtfully placed on the cottage doorsteps for them by scared occupants who wanted protection from adverse spells.

Blamed by her grand-daughter for having made her a witch and accused by her daughter, Old Demdike **confessed** what was expected of a witch, to a local magistrate, Roger Nowell, at his home, Read Hall, on 2nd April, 1612. Twenty years earlier, she told him, while on her way home from begging she had met, near a stonepit, in Goldshaw in Pendle 'a spirit or Devil in the shape of a boy, the one half of his coat black and the other brown, who bade her stay, saying that if she would **give him her soul** she would have anything that she would request'.

The spirit's name was Tibb. Later he appeared to her 'in the likeness of a brown dog, forced himself onto her knee to get blood from under her left arm'. This was just **one of the Devil's disguises**. In 1612 the Pendle witches had encountered spirits in the shape of a man, a dog, a hare and bear. Ann Whittle, known as Chattox, another witch, confessed to having eaten and drunk a diabolical meal with Demdike and two spirits called Tibb and Fancy. They ate well but at the end of it 'they were never fuller nor the better for the same'.

Today we call such stories creations of a deranged mind. We'd say they were barmy. But the **confessions** were treated seriously enough at the time.

People lived in fear of witches to such a degree that they went to great lengths to protect their homes from them. All manner of **anti-witch devices** were used, from special herbs placed above the threshold to holed stone amulets worn as bracelets and necklaces or placed behind the house and barn doors to protect humans and animals alike. Witch balls were hung in the windows to drive away evil spirits and witch posts covered with anti-witch devices were used to protect houses. New House Farm, Rawtenstall, had one. **Witch bottles** were also frequently used; but perhaps the most popular method and certainly the one which has survived the longest and is still in use today was specifically designed for tripping up witches - donkey-stoning doorsteps.

Such devices were usual. But it was unusual for local accusations against suspected or known witches to reach the ears of magistrates that were serious enough to warrant **a trial at quarter sessions or assizes** as happened to the Pendle witches.

It all began on 18th March, 1612, just outside Colne, when John Law, a pedlar from Halifax, refused to give some pins to Alizon Device, grand-daughter of Old Demdike. Alizon was furious with the pedlar, who, as she approached him, had a stroke. His son, Abraham, took the matter to law and Alizon was **charged with witchcraft**, which she later admitted. Not only did she incriminate members of her own family during the trial, she also involved the family of Ann Whittle. As each was tried, more stories of retaliatory witchcraft emerged. According to Alizon, her grand mother, Old Demdike, had bewitched to death the infant son of Richard Baldwin of Weethead because he had not allowed her onto his land. As she was being chased away, Old Demdike promised to pray for him, mentioning him by name several times.

When Ann Whittle was examined, she **admitted** having bewitched Anthony Nutter's cow to death because he preferred Old Demdike to her. There the matter would have rested had not Old Demdike's family and other local witches gathered together at Malkin Tower in Pendle on Good Friday, 1612.

When Roger Nowell of Read heard of the meeting, he made enquiries about it and came to the conclusion that it had been **a conspiracy to blow up Lancaster Castle** and murder the jailer, a Mr. Cowell. In all, nineteen witches were brought to trial, including some from Samlesbury. At the trial the evidence of Jennet Device, the nine year old grand-daughter of Old Demdike, was crucial. **Ten were found guilty of murder** and hanged at Golgotha, Lancaster, on 20th August 1612.

Witches usually came from the poorer parts of the community, but Alice Nutter, one of the Pendle witches was **a rich woman** 'with a great estate and children of good hope'. Elizabeth and James Device accused her of witchcraft and of attending the Malkin Tower meeting. Although she persistently protested her **innocence** she was **executed** with all the others. Little is known of her circumstances but there certainly was a feud between Ann Whittle, or Chattox, and the Nutters, because one of the latter had tried to seduce Ann's daughter. Alice Nutter may have levelled accusations in revenge, even though Ann Whittle and her daughter had already bewitched Robert Nutter, the would be seducer, to death with the aid of a Devil spirit called Fancy.

Man learned very early in his history that the easiest way to transport a heavy load any distance was to **let water take the weight**, providing, of course, that a suitable watercourse was available. Before the construction of good roads and, later, railways, water remained the most **economical and practical** way to transport goods to distant parts of the country. They were taken to the nearest river, floated down to the sea, perhaps there transferred to a sea-going vessel, then carried round the coast and up the river nearest to the intended destination. **Ports** arose at river mouths for this very purpose, and as overseas trade developed the obvious route for goods produced or manufactured inland was down the rivers to the deep-sea ports.

But what if there wasn't a handy river, or the local rivers were too shallow, or too fast, or too narrow for navigation? Inventive minds of the mid-C18th and early-C19th centuries saw the answer in **hand-made, purpose-built rivers** between industrial areas and the main natural river navigations. They engineered canals; they overcame gradients by devising **locks** to raise the horizontal stretches of water and their boats in steps, and they built **aqueducts** to take the new canals over valleys and rivers, and tunnels to avoid the necessity of climbing over or round and biggest hills.

The first canal - the Bridgewater - opened in 1761, and quickly showed itself to be a vast improvement on the alternative appalling roads of the time. A **network** soon began to spread throughout the country, dug laboriously with spade and wheelbarrow by the **'navigators'**, the first 'navvies'. The fact that the Bridgewater had immediately halved the cost of goods carried, particularly coal, did not go unnoticed either, and there was no shortage of financial backers for ever more canals, and the various designs of long, **narrow boats**, towed by horses plodding along the tow-paths, became familiar sights.

The building of canals across the South Pennines undoubtedly facilitated the early **expansion of the wool and cotton industries**, but the coming of the railways cut their usefulness down in its prime. They remain, however, in differing stages of decay and restoration, providing opportunities for recreation on and alongside the waterways - and often in the most beautiful and peaceful of settings.

THE HUDDERSFIELD NARROW CANAL
This unique waterway, almost 20 miles (32 kms) long, extends from Huddersfield, where it is now connected by a culvert to the Broad Canal, over the Pennines to Ashton-Under-Lyne and is the highest canal in Britain.

It relied entirely on **reservoirs** for its water and, in the interests of conserving water, its **74 locks** were constructed as narrow ones like many of those in the Midlands. Given the royal assent in 1794, it was opened in 1811 to become the **second trans-Pennine waterway** connecting Lancashire and Yorkshire.

By far the the greatest **obstacle** on its route was the **steeply rising land** at Standedge. This was overcome by the building of a tunnel which, at 3 miles 135 yards (5 kms) became the **longest tunnel in Britain**. It was 195 metres (645 ft) above sea level and cost £160,000 to build.

Like so many other canals built at that time, it never realised its full potential because, **as trade was building up, the railways arrived.** Narrow boats worked on the Canal from the Cheshire area, including the Peak Forest, Macclesfield, and Trent and Mersey Canals.

The **Huddersfield Broad Canal** had short locks so either the cargos of the conventional narrow boats had to be unloaded or transhipped in Huddersfield. To overcome this problem **shortened versions** of the narrow boat were built and they were able to work both the Huddersfield Broad and Narrow Canals. This limited their cargo carrying capacity but the shorter narrow boats fulfilled a need. They continued to be built until 1911.

The Canal was **abandoned in 1944**, although the last vessel to manage a crossing was in 1948. The lock gates were removed in the 1950s. It is no longer open, even for the occasional inspection boat. Apart from the 42 locks on the Yorkshire side that raise the canal some 133 metres (438 feet) from Huddersfield there are **four aqueducts**.

Between Slaithwaite and Marsden there is an easy 3½ miles (5½ kms) amble along a **recently restored section** of canal where wheelchairs can easily negotiate the all-weather, surfaced towpath.

THE LEEDS AND LIVERPOOL CANAL The first of three trans-Pennine waterways to be started and the last to be finished, the Leeds and Liverpool, has the **longest main route** of any canal in Britain, stretching for 127 miles (204 kms) between Leeds and Liverpool. It was built to open up a through route from Merseyside to the West Riding of Yorkshire and, via the Aire and Calder Navigation, to Humberside. The estimated building cost was £260,000; the final cost was just over £824,000. It is the **only trans-Pennine waterway still open**.

Seventy five years ago Burnley was the world's leading cotton-weaving town. The surrounding area, known as **'the Weavers' Triangle'**, was at the heart of the frenetic activity that accompanied this prosperity; and it was the Leeds and Liverpool Canal that provided the thread around which the harsh life of the cotton workers was woven.

At 148 metres (487 feet) above sea level, the summit of the Leeds and Liverpool was **lower** than the other two Pennine routes. There are **91 locks** along its full length and two tunnels, one almost a mile long at Foulridge and a shorter one at Burnley. At one point it runs along an embankment which reaches a height of 18 metres (60 feet) and it crosses a lot of viaducts. The largest reservoir providing water for it is in the hills above Foulridge tunnel.

Vessels up to a length of 19 metres (62 feet) and with a 4.3 metre (14 feet 2 inch) beam can pass through the locks, including the staircase ones which are usually arranged in twos and threes on the Yorkshire side, the most impressive being **the Bingley Five Rise** which lifts the canal 18 metres (60 feet).

Short boats with a draught of 114 centimetres (3 feet 9 inches) worked the system throughout, carrying some 45 tons each. They were decorated with **delicate scroll work** in subdued colours, compared with which the boats on the Midlands canals were positively garish. Passenger boats plied the Yorkshire section between Bingley and Gargrave in 1791 and between Leeds and Bingley in 1793, **drawn by horses**, which were used exclusively until the 1870s when steam came on the scene. Boats carrying passengers worked the canal, on local workings, until the 1950s. The **largest** amount of traffic ever carried in one year was 2,220,468 tons in 1838.

The Leeds and Liverpool passes through some **magnificent moorland scenery** and is very **popular** as a cruising waterway for both private and hire pleasure craft, with much to offer nature lovers, fishermen, walkers and boating enthusiasts alike.

THE ROCHDALE CANAL The Rochdale Canal was opened throughout in 1804. John Rennie surveyed its route and William Jessop was the canal's engineer. It linked the Calder and Hebble Navigation in the east with the Bridgewater in the west, providing, for the first time, a water route that enabled vessels to travel **from Hull to Liverpool.** The canal is 37 miles (59.5 kms) long and has 92 locks.

The Weaver flat-boats were too long for the locks on the Calder and Aire Navigation and had **to tranship** at Sowerby Bridge; but the keels could travel throughout without any problems. In the 1820s more than 400,000 tons a year were transported on the Rochdale Canal and by the 1830s this had risen to **900,000 tons per annum**. Coal, grain and wool were by far the largest consignments but every type of general cargo was carried.

In 1921 the Rochdale Canal Company ceased to carry in its own craft and this resulted in the final withdrawal of traffic. The **last loaded vessel** to travel the full length of the Canal from east to west was in 1938. On the Lancashire side, traffic remained until the 1950s. Apart from a 1½ mile (2½ kms) section in the middle of Manchester that connected the Ashton Canal with the Bridgewater Canal, the waterway was **abandoned** in 1952.

The canal passes through superb Pennine scenery in its Yorkshire section, from which it descends to Littleborough, in Lancashire, through **a series of 12 locks.** The **Rochdale Canal Society** is doing a tremendous, worthwhile job with **restoration work.** Many parts of the Canal have been culverted and built over; but despite this, work goes on to restore the locks so that eventually craft will again be able to pass along **the whole length** of the canal. This is a long term project; it will take several years but the will is there.

Meanwhile those of you who wish to explore the canal on foot may do so; and sections of towpath are suitable for wheelchairs.

Steam as a source of power had a most dramatic effect on the landscape of the South Pennines. It heralded the **coming of the railways** and better transport. This, in turn, stimulated a rash of growth alongside them. Steam-powered machinery required even larger premises to make full use of its capabilities and investment; and **bigger mills** meant **more employees** and this led to a surge in the building of houses and other associated buildings near the mills. Urbanisation spread, trade increased, more railways were built and the population doubled and re-doubled.

Local government belatedly caught up with this seemingly endless growth and gradually the **Victorian virtues** of regularity, sobriety, and sanitation were introduced. The sheer energy unleashed during this period, with its resultant vigorous mix of mills, terraced houses, weaving sheds, chimneys, chapels, public buildings and pollution created a **uniquely Pennine landscape**.

Three trans-Pennine railways were built alongside the earlier constructed canals and, as with the canal builders, the railway engineers excelled themselves and overcame the **massive physical obstacles** the Pennines presented.

A tunnel, brick lined and 2,638 metres (2,885 yards) long, was cut through the hills between Littleborough and Todmorden on the Manchester to Halifax line. The vertical shafts visible on the hillside above the tunnel are 98 metres (321 feet) deep.

In the Colne Valley at Marsden the Standedge Tunnel was dug parallel to the earlier canal tunnel. **Two thousand navvies** were involved, working in the most appalling conditions. It extended for 3 miles 62 yards (some 5 kms) and was opened in 1849.

The 'Blackburn, Burnley, Accrington and Colne Extension Railway' linked North East Lancashire towns with Manchester, Liverpool and Leeds, via Skipton, as **local industrialists** took every opportunity to increase the output of cloth.

The 'Manchester, Bury and Rossendale Railway' linked up in 1844 and by 1853 extended through the narrow valley from Rawtenstall to Bacup. In 1870 a line opened from Rochdale to the stone quarries at Facit, climbing **very steep gradients** and crossing a picturesque 32 metre (105 foot) viaduct across Healey Dell to reach 305 metres (1,000) feet above sea level. Many **spectacular viaducts** were built and there are some fine examples at Hewenden, near Haworth, and at Brownhills Visitor Centre at Saddleworth, near Oldham.

By 1914 the textile industry had reached the peak of its prosperity, but the period following the First World War was one of **gradual economic decline** as the effect of competition from abroad and revolutionary changes were felt by the textile industry. Some mills switched to new synthetic fabrics, like rayon and nylon, others to satisfying the increasing demand for carpets, furnishings and leisure clothes. Cleaner electric power replaced dirty coal boilers, automation increased and working conditions improved. As more people and goods were carried by road, so the railways declined and eventually many lines were closed.

After the Second World War, further widespread decline in textile manufacturing left owners bankrupt, workers and machinery redundant and buildings obsolete and empty.

With the building industry ailing, stone quarries closed, with no attempt being made to cover the scars on the countryside. The Rochdale-Bacup line stopped operating and the Rochdale and Huddersfield canals became very neglected, some stretches being filled in and the locks removed.

On the **positive** side, heather, birch and gorse recolonised many quarries and old railway lines became excellent walkways and havens for wildlife.

One of the biggest recent changes to the landscape has been **the demolition** of hundreds of mill chimneys. Views of Pennine towns like Burnley, Colne or Halifax, for example, are very different today from those of the 1950s.

Although textiles were in decline, the 50s, 60s and 70s were boom years for Britain generally and brought about lasting alterations to the area. There was an upsurge of **housing estates**, many of which were sadly out of character with the Pennine landscape and the places to which they were attached. **Electricity pylons** strode across some moorland skylines as the National Grid expanded. New reservoirs like Scammonden were built and increased road traffic led to the construction of the **M62** across the South Pennines.

Nevertheless, by the mid-70s, things were beginning to look better for the South Pennines.

Much thought was given to means of stopping the decline and decay, of stimulating and vitalising the economy locally through a number of **enterprising projects and schemes** and of fostering a new type of industry - tourism, with all its ancillary sources, services and craft opportunities.

Local authorities, voluntary groups and private individuals, often helped by government agencies, embarked on **projects** aimed at improving buildings, restoring important features, creating new leisure facilities and opportunities for informal recreation and generally boosting the morale of the South Pennines.

The **Clean Air Acts** of the 50s and 60s removed the atmospheric pollution that had produced the 'dark satanic mills' and local authorities began to clean important civic, commercial and industrial buildings, frequently revealing a richness of architecture that had remained hidden beneath layers of industrial grime 100 years thick.

Traditional weavers' cottages and Pennine farmhouses have been **renovated and occupied** by people who work in nearby cities but who find the rural charm of the South Pennines attractive enough to want to live there.

Increasing **interest in industrial archaeology** and the potential leisure industry has led voluntary groups and local councils to look at the feasibility of restoring both the long forgotten trans-Pennine canals and, to a degree, the age of steam.

The rural branch line which once served the mills along the Worth Valley from Keighley to Oxenhope has been lovingly **restored** by an enthusiastic Preservation Society run by volunteers. A regular steam train service is operating and the restored period stations along the line include Keighley, Damens and Oakworth. There is a **new Vintage Carriage Museum** at Ingrow, a locomotive yard and shop at Haworth and a Keighley and Worth Valley Railway Museum at Oxenhope. This was the line used as the set for the famous 'The Railway Children' film.

The **East Lancashire Railway** is also being restored, with Rossendale recreating an exciting era in public transport. Steam trains, in all their magnificent smoky splendour, have now made a spectacular return to Rawtenstall and this has completed a railway link between Bury Transport Museum and Bolton Street Station.

Already Ramsbottom is enjoying **a tourism boom** through its reopened station and, when Rawtenstall station came on the line in May 1990, the aspirations of the group behind the scheme - the East Lancashire Preservation Society - that **trips into the past** on steam driven trains would be just the ticket for steam enthusiasts were justified.

A regular steam service now runs each Saturday and Sunday between Ramsbottom and Bury. Rossendale Borough Council has supported **the Railway Preservation Society** by forming a Civic Amenities Sub-Committee to help bring back steam trains to the Irwell Valley.

The steam train, with passengers sharing a carriage with **nostalgia**, is but one of the many best features of the past eras that are being **preserved and adapted** to new uses in the South Pennines, but during the dramatic changes of the past 150 years much has been lost. The landscape, under pressure from social and economic as well as natural forces, **changes** constantly and the South Pennines of today is considerably different from the South Pennines of 50, 100, 200 and 300 years ago. It is not practical to resist all changes; and as the area enters a new century the landscape will continue to **evolve** in response to new social and economic factors. The growth of tourism and leisure and the marketability of the region's heritage are all good signs that the landscape will develop in a positive way that conserves the past and reflects **the uniqueness** of the South Pennines' character and identity.

The Standing Conference of South Pennine Authorities is to be **congratulated** on the splendid way it has **co-ordinated the area's potential** and made people aware of what it has to offer. Thanks largely to **SCOSPA**, the future of the South Pennines is assured and, for the prospective visitor, has never been brighter. The South Pennine story is indeed a success story.

North of the Aire Gap lie the limestone hills of the Yorkshire Dales; south of Chapel-en-le-Frith lie the limestone heights of the Derbyshire Peaks. Squeezed between them is a huge chunk of **Millstone Grit**, the bedrock of the South Pennines.

Whereas limestone carries a very thin **soil**, that in the high fells of the Millstone Grit area is sandy and acid. Limestone is soluble in water and charged with carbon dioxide, which keeps the soil light and crumbly. This, along with free drainage, keeps the soil comparatively dry, even during periods of prolonged rain.

The Grit which covers most of the South Pennines forms a sandy soil entirely deficient in calcium. This enables organic matter to accumulate, drainage becomes impeded, the soil becomes wet and sticky and it usually has a thick cover of peat.

Unlike the grits, the Millstone **shales** are rarely found on the summits. They are found on the slopes of hills where they slide to form belts of heavy soil along the lower flanks. This is well suited to supporting thick woodland.

Millstone Grit is a rugged **rock** and because of its durability it is often exposed above gaps left by the more easily weathered softer rocks, giving it its strange shapes. Many of these odd looking rocks have attracted local names like the 'Druid's Stone', the 'Nab' and 'Catstones'.

Throughout the South Pennines **scarps** stand proud against the sky. They are the result of the Millstone Grit being folded under **tremendous pressure** and then subjected to centuries of weathering. Raised areas were developed that, for the most part, sloped gently eastwards and had steep, westerly facing bluffs. Good examples of this feature are Blackstone Edge, Standedge, Pule Hill and Castle Hill.

The **rivers** starting high up in the base of the Millstone Grit descend steeply, cutting down into the lower strata, and resulting from this are many lovely waterfalls which feature prominently in the South Pennines. Once below the lower strata the river courses become less steep and, as they cut through younger and younger rocks, change their valley shapes accordingly, so that no two valleys or any two parts of any single valley are alike.

The base of the Millstone Grit frequently contains thin **coal seams**, accounting for coal pits near the summits of the fells, mostly from the C18th and early C19th but the real coal measures of the greater coal fields which lie along the eastern flank of the Pennines are not as old as the Millstone Grit. They are spread above the Millstone Grit which thereabouts dips and disappears beneath them.

Peat covers about 60 square miles (155 sq kms) of the South Pennines, lying at an average depth of 9 metres (30 feet). It consists of **plant material** which has been preserved in air-free conditions which are best found in a very wet bog. Time changes vegetation into humic material in which many plant structures, in particular pollen and seeds from nearby woodlands, remain in remarkably fresh condition. From this it has been established that, following the scouring of the Ice Age, a steady **return of trees** to the South Pennines, and other upland areas, produced thick forest cover on these uplands.

Around 500 BC, when the climate became much **wetter and colder,** the tree cover died off on the higher fells and bogs and a peat cover quickly spread.

This harsh climate lasted throughout the Roman occupation and was followed by a **very dry period**, from the C6th to the C9th during which the Anglo-Danish woodland clearances were made in the valleys and lower lands.

The cold, wet climatic periods were responsible for the growth and spread of '**blanket peat**' across nearly all the fells above 305 metres (1,000 feet) and killed much of the highest forest. Unregulated sheep breeding completed the destruction, even in the valley heads.

Today's **climatic conditions** are closely related to the topography and the contrast between the exposed fell tops and the sheltered valley bottoms is wide, even though only short distances separate one from the other.

Split a piece of Millstone Grit and the ores in it sparkle **orange and gold,** but, no matter how fresh, they soon oxidise in the air and darken, so Millstone Grit never looks clean. Yet it is because Millstone Grit is so durable that the bleak cotton and wool processing mill towns were able to come into being.

ASHWORTH VALLEY/CHEESDEN BROOK Sited some three miles west of Rochdale, south of the A680, this is a very popular **rambling area** through wooded valleys and open moorland. It contains historical remains, trails and a great variety of flora and fauna.

CASTLE HILL Providing one of the North's **best panoramas,** Castle Hill is one of the finest examples of an Iron Age hill fort in the country. The hill, just south of Huddersfield, is now crowned by the Jubilee Tower, built in 1898.

CALDER VALLEY An area of high sided valleys and waterfalls with tributary streams eroding deeper valleys or cloughs.

HARDCASTLE CRAGS North east of Hebden Bridge, this beautiful **wooded valley** is owned by the National Trust.

HARDEN BECK By following Harden Beck from the Brown Cow at Keelham to the Malt Shovel at Harsden, with one eye on the time, you will be able to enjoy **a pint at each pub** and a delightful walk. There are two reservoirs in the valley where dinghy sailing takes place and waterfowl gather. In Golt Stock there are pleasant **woods** and **waterfalls** and the graceful Hewenden Viaduct is most impressive.

HEALEY DELL NATURE RESERVE This is a breath-taking **gorge with waterfalls,** moss covered ruins, stone arches spanning the River Snodden and a stone viaduct soaring out of the woods, with an unbelievably rich variety of plants and animals. The Nature Reserve covers 40 hectares (100 acres) and a warden provides a good information service to visitors.

MARSDEN MOOR This huge area of open moorland straddling the A62 and A620 constitutes one of the **largest single tracts of National Trust land** in England. The area includes nationally important engineering works and transport routes, the well preserved Rapes Highway packhorse route, a Site of Special Scientific Interest at Pule Hill and a stretch of the Pennine Way.

OGDEN WATER Between Halifax and Haworth, just west of the A629, Ogden Water is an area of **mixed woodland** and **open moorland** centred around **a reservoir**. It is being developed for informal recreation.

PIETHORNE VALLEY Piethorne Valley is tucked into Bleakedgate Moor with the A672 on its eastern side and the A640 along its southern edge. The M62 wraps around it to the north and west. Containing a series of six very different reservoirs, it is a Nature Reserve in which tremendous interest has been aroused by the flora and fauna of the valley, together with the archaeological excavations at Rag Hole. On Watergrove Reservoir the main activities are **dinghy sailing and wind surfing.** The **Trail** around the Reservoir and the surrounding hills passes through upland farms and abandoned hamlets. Whatever the season, the **upland scenery** is exhilarating.

SADDLEWORTH MOOR Saddleworth is a **lovely moor** on which lie the isolated hamlets of Delph, Diggle, Denshaw and Dobcross, now linked through a series of local interest trails. This is fine walking country which offers many opportunities for both keen ramblers and gentle strollers, using paths by the River Tame and the Huddersfield Narrow Canal. Uppermill, the largest village on Saddleworth Moor, has cafes, a craft centre and a museum. A visit to the **Brownhill Visitor Centre** will enable you to pick up details of local guided walks. Here there is an **impressive viaduct** which carries the railway over a wood and a canal and the river runs under them all. The Chew Valley Tramway Trail is at Saddleworth and is well worth walking. Go on : have a go.

SHIPLEY GLEN Baildon. A cable tramway, built in 1895, hauls visitors up through Walker Wood to the top of the Glen, with its fine rock formations, Countryside Centre and other attractions.

TOWNELEY PARK - HURSTWOOD - WORSTHORNE MOOR It is here that the Pennine hills intrude into Burnley; and from here you are able to look into Yorkshire from the Pennine Ridge. A variety of **moorland walks** spread from Hurstwood village and, through an access agreement with the North West Water Authority, Worsthorne Moor is now available to explore.

WYCOLLER COUNTRY PARK A diverse landscape which embraces enclosed pasture land, hidden valleys and open moorland. The Park is centred on the intriguing old weaving hamlet tucked into Wycoller Dean, which is ideally suited as a base from which to explore the surrounding countryside.

The **great upland forests** which once covered some sixty square miles of the South Pennines had vanished by 2,000 years BC. A few remnants remained but these were confined to the lower lying cloughs associated...... sheltered and narrow valleys. On the exposed tops, the decaying trees and other plant life formed over many centuries **a layer of peat** that spread across the Millstone Grit bedrock like a thick skin 9 metres (30 feet) deep.

Black and fibrous peat favours low soil temperature and waterlogging of the soil, which deprives it of oxygen. The peat of the South Pennines is a **bog peat** and is of two types, a 'raised' bog peat formed in hollows, mainly from sphagnum moss, and a blanket bog peat which is found on sloping ground and is derived in acid soil mainly from grass and sedge.

Cotton grass abounds on these moorland bogs, its white and fluffy seed heads adding colour and interest to these lonely heights. **Bilberry and heather,** both acid lovers, are also found there. Bell heather tends to keep to drier parts of the South Pennines. That found around the bogs is **ling,** which for many hundreds of years has been useful for bedding, fuel, thatching and basketry. This versatile plant also yields an orange dye and has been used to flavour beer.

Red grouse, unique to Britain, rely for their food almost entirely on ling heather, eating different parts of the plant from winter until its seeds are full in the autumn. The cock birds mark out their territory in a dramatic display. They leap into the air with spread wings and descend steeply again, extending their necks and feet and fanning their tails; and they challenge rival cocks with their barking call: 'Go Bak, go bak, bak, bak.' Birds which cannot establish a well-heathered territory often fall victim to disease or predators.

Hard winters on the high South Pennines can often make life very difficult for the red grouse, which may have to spend long spells treading with their feet to avoid being buried in **drifting snow.** Snow often falls in April when the female is laying eggs; but even if the eggs are badly frosted, the grouse chicks rarely fail to hatch.

The poor, waterlogged soils of the South Pennines tops do not contain the nutrients most plants need for survival, but a notable exception is the **sundew** (*drosera rotundifolia*) which has adapted to these spartan conditions by becoming carnivorous. Its leaves are covered in red, spiky hairs which are used to **catch insects** when they settle. These are digested and absorbed through the leaves and this is how the sundews receive their food. The sundew's flowers rarely open and are usually found in bud form.

Other plants that are at home in the South Pennines bog land are the **bog-asphodel**, the bog pimpernel and the butterwort or bog violet. The bog-asphodel is a very useful plant. In the Shetlands it has frequently been used instead of saffron for both medicine and dyeing. After flowering, the flower heads turn a deep saffron colour. **Bog pimpernel,** seen mainly on the western side of the South Pennines, carries pale flowers on creeping stems. **Butterwort** is a strange plant. It over winters as a rootless bud. It is said that milk from a cow that has eaten butterwort will protect a new born child. None of these plants is as common as it was a century ago because of draining operations.

The heather moors of the South Pennines are by no means all the same. **Ilkley Moor** is predominantly a heather moor renowned for its red grouse. It supports other bird life too, including kestrel, curlew, lapwing, skylark and short-eared owl. Moreover, being an urban common it is easily accessible and has a good network of footpaths crossing it.

Haworth Moor is a Site of Special Scientific Interest. It is an example of a heather moorland being managed for grouse production and supporting an associated bird life, including birds of prey and waders.

Worsthorne Moor is a cotton grass moor. Purple moor grass and mat grass dominate the slopes. On the tops, a carpet of cotton grass supports curlew, golden plover and other associated bird life. **Uncontrolled fires** have taken off some of the peat cover on the upper slopes, exposing the underlying gritstone.

Lishworth Moor is an extensive water catchment area to the south of the A68 and here the RSPB has established a **peregrine watch** to assist the return of this magnificent bird of prey to our hills.

The moorland ecosystem supports bird **populations** that depend on insects, vegetation and mammals for their existence. These are birds that prefer exposed open spaces to the shelter of the valleys and nest on the ground rather than in trees, hedges or buildings. Most of these birds are highly mobile and **migrate** to warmer climates in winter. For example, wading birds, like the dunlin, golden plover and curlew leave the cotton grass bogs in August and head for the estuaries, like the Dee, where they feed on the mud flats. Other birds, like the ring ouzel, fly abroad to winter in the sun. Those ground nesting birds which do winter on the moors, mainly grouse, camouflage themselves by changing their plumage with the seasons, thus protecting themselves from predators. Because of this **variability in the bird population,** predators like the fox are not attracted to moorlands as a source of food and, the birds are mostly left undisturbed.

The extremely acidic water of the moorland reservoirs supports very little in the way of **aquatic wild life**; but reservoirs offer a temporary home to some birds like the Canada geese.

The South Pennine **woodlands** are, on the whole, in rather a sorry state. Since medieval times man has cleared a large section of woodland for agriculture. The industrial development of the last century has also had some effect. Woodland is now mainly found in the smaller, steeper, less accessible cloughs. Many of the larger and more noticeable deciduous woodlands are the product of estate management by wealthy landowners in past centuries or managed by bodies like the National Trust. There are relatively **few coniferous plantations** in the South Pennines. Those which exist have mostly been planted around water supply reservoirs with pine, larch and Norway spruce the main species.

Mostly it is **sessile oak** that covers the South Pennines cloughs, in some accounting for over 90% of the trees. Other trees usually found growing alongside them are birch, ash, rowan and holly with some alder and willow growing in wetter areas or on stream banks. The exposed position of many woodlands results in **poorly developed trees**. Many cloughs now contain a sizeable representation of species which are not native to Northern England. These are mainly sycamore and beech. The deep shade cast by **beech trees** prevents the establishment of most ground flora, except perhaps ferns. This effect is exacerbated by the beech tree roots, which are shallow and themselves limit the growth of other plants. Many local woodlands were felled for the war effort earlier in the century and re-planting has been carried out in various areas. This regenerated woodland is a mixture of sycamore, ash and birch, with the sycamore being dominant.

The larger and less accessible clough woodlands are locally important for wildlife, particularly breeding birds. The **common woodland species** like blackbirds, thrushes and tits are often joined by other less widespread species like the green and greater spotted woodpeckers, willow warblers, blackcaps and chiff chaffs.

Where the **woodlands** are fenced and the soil is less acidic, **wild flowers** like the herb robert, dogs mercury, wood sorrel and pink purslain are able to grow. With these exceptions, most cloughs are carpeted on their lower slopes by creeping soft grass. Bluebells also often grow there, being able to develop and flower in spring before the main period of grass growth. On **the upper slopes** of the cloughs, the soils are more acidic, the nutrients having been washed out. Here the dominant ground cover is wavy hair grass which, in turn, is often replaced with bilberry and heather on the upper slopes of the clough. The largest area of clough woodland in the South Pennines is Hardcastle Crags. The trees are mainly deciduous with some conifers, mostly Scots pine. The range of associated woodland wildflowers and birds is wide. Run by the National Trust, it has three colour-coded Nature Trails to explore.

Oak dominates **Houghton Hagg**, a 7 hectare (17 acre) woodland, with some sycamore and ash. The woodland includes a coppice woodland with an associated wide range of wild flowers.

Healey Dell is a **clough oak woodland** with a variety of acidic grassland and heath habitats.

North Dean, owned by Calderdale MBC, is a **well managed woodland** with a profusion of oak and beech along the valley side. There are some 4 miles (6½ kms)of trails.

One of the most endearing features of the South Pennines landscape is its **patchwork quilt of fields,** each a different shade of green and divided by dry stone walls.

The Enclosure Acts of the C18th and C19th led to unprecedented activity in **wall construction** in the South Pennines and through it much moorland edge land was claimed for pasture. At about this time most of the distinctive farm houses and barns were built.

At that time, the South Pennines landscape was much different and it was still profitable to grow **cereal crops** on the more sheltered fields. Signs of this can be clearly seen in favourable light conditions, like ridge and furrow patterns appearing on some fields which have not seen a plough for a century. A steady decline in the profitability of hill farming coupled with an increase in the costs of walling has taken its toll. Traditional enclosures are slowly being replaced by easily maintained **fences,** and fields on the moorland edge are being invaded by soft rush and poor grasses like cocksfoot and tufted hair grasses.

All enclosed fields in the South Pennine uplands are given over to **grazing** at some time of the year. But there the similarity between fields ends.The farmer needs a **range of crops** to keep his animals fed throughout the year. The more productive fields are those most sheltered from the often harsh conditions experienced in these uplands, where even a small difference in height on the same slope can make a great difference to the rate of grass growth. Generally, the **sheltered fields** are managed most intensively, growth being encouraged by applications of lime and fertilisers, which encourage the highly competitive grasses. Herbicides are applied to keep thistles and other unwanted plants under control. Fields where this happens are known as '**mowing meadows**' and are left mostly ungrazed during the summer months. Sometimes they are cut twice to provide silage feed for those animals kept inside during the winter. Some farmers **plough up** their best meadows for reseeding with perennial rye grass, with clover often being included in the seed mixtures. The reasoning behind this is to exploit clover's value in 'fixing' nitrogen in the soil, thus saving money on other sources of nitrogen, the artificial fertilizers.

The plant that survives best above 610 metres (2,000 feet) is cotton-grass. It takes over in the bogs, especially on the thick, poorly drained peat, and its cotton like seed tufts whiten the moor. Areas where it is prolific should be avoided because the ground on which it grows is usually treacherous. Where sphagnum moss grows emerald green, it usually covers a very dangerous patch of deep bog - another area to avoid.

Along the lower edges of the moors there is a broad area of rough pasture comprised of grasses which vary a great deal according to the relative wetness of the ground and its acidity. On highly leached and acid soils, mat grass dominates. It is very coarse and grows in rough clumps. Where a little limestone is present and the acidity drops, sheep fescue abounds and the pasturage is much richer. In the wettish patches around springs and other water seepages, purple moor-grass and rushes hold sway. It is on the edge of the limestone area that the grass of the South Pennines is 'sweetest'.

Despite Government incentives to farmers to improve their grasslands, it is still possible to find **old fashioned hay meadows** which have a greater selection of grasses and wild flowers. Here may be found yellow rattle, buttercups, yarrow, dogstail and other traditional species that thrive on the acid-to-neutral soils in the South Pennines.

Higher up the valleys, the soils become more acidic, the climate more severe and consequently the effort put into grassland management falls off rapidly. In this valley-rim land of broken walls, sheep eat the more nutritious grasses and this promotes the growth of unwanted species like soft rush and mat grass. So the moor fields are gradually being converted to **rough grazing** and slowly absorbed into the moorland scene.

Most South Pennine **road verges** are narrow and not mown. Often the flora found there is an overspill from nearby fields but, more usually, they have become dominated by 'invasive' plants like cow parsley and hogweed. In the **valleys,** where walls sometimes give way to a softer landscape of hedges, hawthorn predominates and harbours more interesting wild flowers like red campion and herb robert.

Most **gritstone walls** provide a moist surface on which lichens and mosses thrive. On some walls sheltered by trees, ferns and sometimes wild flowers sometimes also become established.

Nature and man working in harness, have produced today's South Pennine landscape, which far from being forbidding and satanic, as propounded mainly by people who have not explored the area, is, in fact, a treasure house brimming with the riches of nature.

ALKRINGTON WOODS NATURE RESERVE TRAIL O/S Ref: SD 864053: Length: 2 miles (3 kms) Manager/owner: Rochdale Metropolitan Borough Council. Woodland Trail. Leaflet available from RMBC. Best season to visit: Spring and early summer.

The trail is laid out in an area of **beech woodland,** varied with oak and birch. The soil is sandy and badly drained, thus giving dry spreads of bracken contrasted with shallow pools and boggy patches. There is the additional interest of the **river bank**. A good range of woodland birds frequents the area.

HEALD WOOD O/S Ref: SD 936349 : Area: 2.2 hectares (5½ acres) Manager/owner: Woodland Trust. Deciduous woodland. Best season to visit: Spring and summer.

The **wood** contains beech, oak, ash and elm, and slopes steeply **down to the riverside** areas along Pendle Water where there is an interesting variety of plants.

HEALEY DELL O/S Ref: SD 883159: Area 70 hectares (175 acres). Manager/owner: Rochdale Borough Council Reserve. Narrow moorland-edge valley. Nature trail booklet available from warden's hut or RBC. Best season to visit: Spring and early summer.

The valley opens to the south and thus is warmer and more **sheltered** than surrounding land, a circumstance which encourages a rich variety of ferns, mosses and liverworts. **Woodlands** hang above the water, adding to the shade and the humidity, providing suitable conditions for ladyfern and lemon scented fern, while the hard rocks are acid enough for hard fern. The woods themselves are varied with ancient oak and birch woodland and planted trees, mostly sycamores.

The ground cover under the older woods is typical of acid moor edge sites with heather and bilberry, wavy hair grass and tormentil. Open areas are thick with bracken while the trees tend to be widely spread and small. Below the woodland a **disused railway line crosses the river** by a viaduct on which grows the locally uncommon hart's tongue. The ballast for the line was the limestone gravel, the presence of which has allowed an unexpected range of lime-loving plants to colonise the valley.

The **wetter areas,** where the nutrients are easiest to absorb, tend to be the richest parts of any site. Healey Dell is no exception and the damper parts have a wide variety of wetland plants. An interesting range of hybrids of both southern and northern marsh-orchid with common spotted orchid may also be seen.

Birds of woodland, scrubland, open fields and water occur, together with passage migrants and seasonal visitors. **Butterfly records** are sparse but moths are plentiful and include flame shoulder and true lovers' knot.

HOLLINGWORTH LAKE COUNTRY PARK. O/S ref: SD939153: area: 84 hectares (210 acres) Manager/owner: Rochdale Metropolitan Borough Council. Large reservoir. Best season to visit: Winter.

The **lakeside trail** provides excellent views across the water at any time of the year but winter is likely to be best for water birds, when disturbance is at its lowest. A **closed sanctuary** holds a variety of breeding birds in summer.

LAUND CLOUGH O/S Ref: SD770274: Area: 2 hectares (5 acres). Manager/owner: Woodland Trust. Deciduous woodland. Best season to visit: Spring and summer.

This important area of **amenity woodland** lies on a steep sided valley close to houses, and contains a variety of mature broad leaved trees.

TANDLE HILL COUNTRY PARK O/S Ref: SD 907087: Area 44 hectares (110 acres). Manager/owner: Oldham Metropolitan Borough Council. Grassland and woodland. Best season to visit: Spring and early summer.

A nature trail within the country park demonstrates the interest of the **grassy hillside** crowned with beech and conifers.

WYCOLLER COUNTRY PARK O/S Ref: SD 926395: Area: 141 hectares (352 acres). Manager/owner: Lancashire County Council. Moor-edge country park. Nature trail leaflet from site or LCC. Best season to visit: Early summer.

This attractive river valley area lies in the old Forest of Trawden, a most appealing place to explore.

Farming in the South Pennines

The first South Pennines farmers were semi-nomadic. They kept to the hilltops whenever possible because the swampy, thickly wooded valley bottoms were unhealthy, uninviting and difficult to defend. So they kept to the safer high ground, felling trees for clearings around their dwellings, farming the soil until it was exhausted and moving on. The only effect this had on the landscape was to accelerate soil erosion in the poorer areas. This allowed cotton grass, sphagnum moss and other poor vegetation to encroach. In time, large areas of moorland became waterlogged and this led to a build-up of peat.

The Romans assiduously avoided the South Pennines, leaving them to the remaining Celtic communities. Not until the Angles, the Danes and the Norsemen came and established farmsteads did South Pennine agriculture advance to any appreciable degree.

During the Norman invasion and after the C11th, the new feudal lords ran their large South Pennine holdings from more hospitable, distant places like Skipton and Clitheroe. These holdings or hunting areas were called forests, although they were not covered entirely by trees. The lords increasingly sought revenue from these bleak areas and sold timber and grazing rights. So cattle rearing became more popular, with large areas called 'vaccaries' being set aside for cattle rearing. In time the hunting areas gradually shrank until, eventually, they became confined to enclosed 'deer parks'.

From the C12th onwards, the hillside settlements continued to grow and communal farming became established on marginal land between the 600 and 1,000 contours. Sheep were grazed for their meat, milk and fleeces, but little mutton was eaten by the farmers themselves.

Until the middle of the C19th when cheap corn imports became widely available, the staple diet was locally grown oats, supplemented by a few root crops. The corn had to be ground in the lord of the manor's mill, which was often sited some distance away, close to a source of water power.

During the C14th, because exposed uplands crop yields were poor and uncertain, some of the farmers began clearing, cultivating and settling the south-facing valley sides and were beginning to clear and drain the valley bottoms.

Farming in the South Pennines has never been easy. Poor land could sustain few cattle and sheep, poor soil gave meagre crop returns and always there was a constant battle with often savage weather.

Frequently, when a farmer died, his land was divided equally amongst his sons and this continual fragmentation of farms left families with less and less to support themselves on; and this, in turn, led to poverty. To help alleviate this distressing state of affairs, some farmers turned to cloth making at home as a second industry. Slowly the most marginal farms were abandoned as the farmers took up weaving as a sole occupation.

During the 1840s, most of the South Pennines farmland was either meadow or pasture for grazing cattle. Sheep were relegated to the poorer moorland pastures; and here large estate owners placed raising grouse above rearing sheep.

South Pennines land is poor and needs much attention but the farmhouses are eagerly sought for conversion and modernisation by part time 'hobby farmers', usually rich city dwellers in need of a second home. Many of them have little or no knowledge of grassland management and the surrounding fields usually go unwanted and uncared for.

The genuine hill farmer today is operating under increasingly marginal conditions. Government subsidies are being cut to conform with Common Market regulations. This means that fewer farms can provide a living for the family without a supplementary income. Here tourism has come to the aid of the South Pennine hill farmer; and today many farms offer bed, breakfast and, often, full-board.

Meanwhile, many upland pastures are reverting to moorland while on the lower slopes the more difficult terrain becomes increasingly overgrown and neglected. The contrast between the lush green fields of the well-husbanded valley sides and the ragged state of the less well-tended ones is evident.

Throughout history, in troubled times, the South Pennines hill farmer has responded to the national need. Now it is the same farmer who is in need of help. If it is not forthcoming, the South Pennines landscape, as we know it, will never be the same again.

For hors d'oeuvres savour this small slice of official **picnic sites and other locations where catering facilities are provided;** and having whetted your appetite you will find that many more equally relishable eating places pepper the South Pennines. Be it epicureanism you seek or simply a humble butty stop, be assured that the South Pennine catering establishments are ever willing to serve. In alphabetical order of South Pennine authorities, these are:

BURNLEY

BURNLEY MECHANICS This thriving **Arts and Entertainments Centre** houses a 427 seat multi-purpose theatre complete with bar and catering facilities. There are meeting rooms on the first and second floors, the Mid-Pennine Arts Association art gallery and workshop on the lower ground floor and Burnley's Tourist Information Centre and a theatre box office on the ground floor.

ROWLEY LAKE This is a man-made lake formed by diverting the course of the River Brun and flooding a section of the valley. The lake, which is **encircled by footpaths**, attracts a variety of water fowl and has been stocked with fish for the angler. There is a picnic site, toilets and parking facilities.

THURSDEN PICNIC SITE This small picnic site overlooks the **wooded valley** of Thursden Brook and provides magnificent views of the surrounding countryside.

TOWNELEY PARK Towneley Park is 115 hectares (284 acres) of beautiful **parkland** containing a Natural History Centre, nature trails, tennis courts, bowling greens, pitch and putt, an 18 hole golf course and the new 9 hole Brunshaw Golf Course, picnic sites and parking.

KIRKLEES

BROWNHILL,RAMSDEN AND DIGLEY RESERVOIRS These reservoirs are on the boundary of the magnificent Peak District National Park. They are well wooded and provide **attractive walks and picnicking.** Nearby is the unspoilt village of Holme above which Holme Moss TV mast forms a well known landmark. The panoramic views from the adjacent A6024 are superb.

SCAMMONDEN RESERVOIR The dam wall of this huge reservoir carries the M62 motorway. The reservoir itself reaches into **spectacular Pennine scenery** with picnic and viewing areas, footpaths, car parks and toilets, a sailing club and activity centre.

OLDHAM

ALEXANDRA CRAFT CENTRE Forty art and craft units, including fine art prints, oriental gifts, knitwear, china, jewellery, books and a picture framing service. See **traditional craftsmen** at work. The coffee is excellent and the baking home-made.

PENDLE

BALL GROVE PICNIC SITE The lake here is used for **coarse fishing.** The season opens in mid June and closes in mid March and there are facilities for the disabled angler as well as a children's play area. There is easy access to **a beautiful walk** by the riverside to Wycoller. The lake is available for canoeing and sub-aqua diving. There is a restaurant.

BARLEY PICNIC SITE This furnished picnic area is by the village stream and it has a **children's play area.** Its Information Centre provides local history, maps for the motorist and walker, and a wide range of souvenirs. The picnic site is an ideal base for taking a Pendle Hill walk or around two local reservoirs, Black Moss and Ogden, where fishing is available. There are refreshments.

MARSDEN PARK The park is set in **beautiful and wooded surroundings** with crown green bowling, crazy golf, aviary and children's play area. There is an 18 hole golf course. Café facilities are available.

ROCHDALE

LITTLEBOROUGH COACH HOUSE HERITAGE CENTRE Originally a coaching house, the Centre is now a **Heritage and Information Centre**, but also acts as a shop window for local artists and crafts people. Regular exhibitions are held there, Heritage Trails begin there and it has a café.

ROSSENDALE

SKI ROSSENDALE This is the **largest dry ski slope** in England. It has a 180 metres (195 ft) main slope, intermediate and nursery slopes. There is a ski lift, tuition is available and there are both ski shop and lecture room. It is within half a mile of Rawtenstall town centre and has a licensed restaurant.

Have you ever wondered how the world looks to a dog, a fish or a bee? Are you colour blind, and if so how does the world look to you? What is Turkey Red? These are just a few of the questions which are examined by Britain's only museum of colour, the Society of Dyers and Colourists' **Colour Museum**.

Opened in 1978 by Dr Magnus Pyke, it consists of two galleries, the **World of Colour,** which examines the importance, physical nature and use of colour in everyday life; and **Colour and Textiles**, which considers the practical applications of colour in textiles and so recounts the story of dyeing and textile printing from ancient Egypt right up to present day computerised technology.

Because the Museum employs a whole range of media, from traditional show cases and push buttons to computers and audio-visual presentations, both galleries are extremely lively as well as being informative. Quite simply this museum allows visitors to experience colour as never before and proves that learning really can be fun. Indeed, that's probably why it was awarded the title '**Best Industrial Museum 1988**'!

The **Colne Valley Museum**, at Golcar near Huddersfield, is housed in three weavers' cottages with a total of eight rooms crammed with the taste of life in the Colne Valley and the local history of textiles. Once inside the building, the assemblage of fascinating domestic and industrial chattels, from Grandma's corsets to a working Spinning Jenny, capture the visitor in a Victorian time warp. The unique gas-lit clogger's workshop is complete with iron stove and a tale or two from the cloggers, who are only too willing to explain the finer points of 'courtin' clogs'.

The Museum, run by volunteers, specialises in school and party visits, welcomes visitor involvement and is proud that there are few glass cases or roped off areas. It is a place to explore and perhaps learn a craft. In April and October each year, the well established **Craft and Working Weekends** feature local crafts, baking and other demonstrations.

The Museum members are preparing to meet the challenges of the 90s, in particular the increase in tourism in Kirklees, with a touch of true Victorian grit and a dash of Yorkshire humour.

The Yorkshire Mining Museum

Much of the industry in Yorkshire's towns and cities was based on coal and the award-winning **Yorkshire Mining Museum** at Caphouse Colliery assures you of a fascinating day out. Here you can go underground into authentic old workings. The exciting **underground experience** begins in the lamp room, where you collect helmet, lamp and battery. Then with an experienced local miner as your guide, you take your brass check or tally with you as you ride the cage 137 metres (450 feet) to the pit bottom. Along the underground route, displays of models and machines trace the history of this very special industry from the 1820s through to the present day. Once entire families worked together by the light of candles, where now huge modern machines cut the coal.

The underground tour takes approximately one hour, and when you have handed back your check and equipment, there is still lots more to see and do. In the stable block you can find genuine retired pit ponies. There are **many indoor and outdoor exhibits**. For instance, near by is the old boiler house which supplied steam for the 1876 steam winder. This has just been restored to its former glory, and is powered by steam from a new, coal-fired boiler.

The new **Visitor Centre** houses an exhibition gallery with fascinating displays and films, as well as a souvenir shop and licensed cafeteria serving fine, home-cooked food. This C18th colliery nestles in rolling countryside with fine views; there is a lovely on-site nature trail, and an exciting adventure playground is situated in woodlands.

The Yorkshire Mining Museum is on the A642, half way between Wakefield and Huddersfield, close to the M1 and M62. It is open throughout the year (except December 25th, 26th and January 1st) 10am-5pm. Groups of 15 or more are requested to book in advance. Underground access is available for wheelchair users by prior arrangement and there are facilities for the disabled on the surface. Children under 5 are not allowed underground, but are admitted free to the surface, where there is a toddlers' play area. This is a real coal mine, so warm clothes and sensible shoes are advisable but whether you are above or below ground, the Yorkshire welcome is just as warm.

The National Museum of Photography, Film and Television is now the most popular national museum outside London. Its unique recipe for facts and fun, art and science, still and moving pictures draws visitors from all over the world.

Situated in Bradford city centre, the Museum boasts six floors of displays and constantly changing special exhibitions, exploring the media.

At the heart of the building is the **IMAX Auditorium,** its huge screen the height of a five-storey building; vast, brilliant, pin-sharp images sweep you into another world, journeying into the realms of space, the depths of the ocean, wildlife - indeed, any subject big enough to be turned into this extraordinary experience.

Elsewhere in the Museum, visitors can explore the dynamic, changing world of photographs; visit the **Story of Popular Photography**, a massive collection of images and objects donated to the NMPFT by Kodak Limited, and now theatrically re-designed and re-interpreted to tell the story of photography from the point of view of the man in the street.

On view are the world's biggest lens and the smallest snapshot, the first-ever photograph, the most hard-hitting news photographs, and some of the world's most exotic fashion shots.

The Museum features constantly changing special exhibitions. Subjects vary from work of photographic masters like Andre Kertesz, David Hockney and Snowdon to the secrets of television puppeteers like Jim Henson. A **'What's On'** guide outlining the current exhibition programme is available by post from the Marketing Office.

In the celebrated **television galleries**, you can step behind the camera to discover how television is made. This is your opportunity to become a camera-person in the TV drama studio, try your hand at vision mixing; be a newsreader for a day, and see yourself flying on a Magic Carpet over land and sea, courtesy of television's chromakey technique.

The **Education Unit,** one of the busiest in the country, organises workshops and projects for students of all ages. There is also a full programme of theatre, talks and script-to-screen sessions for those who left the classroom long ago.

'Action Replay', the Museum's own in-house theatre company, has introduced live theatre to the Museum galleries, bringing to life some of the stories and personalities who have made photographic history. Performances are free; details are available from the Marketing Office.

And, from winter 1991, you can also see a working television studio in the Museum; TV-AM will open their remote control station from the sixth floor - the only transmitting TV studio to feature in any media museum in the world. It will also function as a walkthrough display.

And, best of all, the fun of a day out at the Museum comes absolutely free - there is a charge only for the IMAX cinema. So do take your opportunity to visit the NMPFT, the Museum for anyone who has ever taken a photograph, been to the cinema or watched television - and nowadays, that means everybody. Indeed, it is hard to think of a Museum subject which could have a more universal application or be of interest to a wider audience than this one.

The Museum is open daily from Tuesday to Sunday, 10.30am-6pm.

IMAX performances are given at 12 noon, 1pm, 2pm, 3pm and 4pm, with an additional performances at 5pm on Saturdays and Sundays. Evening performances are given on Thursdays and Fridays at 7.30pm.

Current IMAX admission charges for a single performance are £3.00, with concessions (available on weekdays only) of £2.00 and £1.50 for children under 16.

Admission charges for IMAX double bill performances are £5.00, with concessions (again on weekdays only) at £3.00 and children under 16 at £2.50.

All prices and details of the programme are subject to change, so please confirm details with the Box Office at the following numbers:

Marketing Office Tel: (0274) 727488, Extension 273; **Box Office** Tel: (0274) 732277; **Education Unit** Tel: (0274) 725347.

HOCKNEYS & HERITAGE

Bradford's Cartwright Hall & Industrial Museum

Described at its 1904 opening as "the finest building in Europe of its kind, with the finest carvings in the world".

This is the magnificent **CARTWRIGHT HALL** — a delightful baroque-style gallery set in its own park, with an important collection of Victorian, Edwardian and Modern art and host to constantly changing contemporary shows.

The lively exhibition programme has something for everyone — from local art clubs, through academic retrospectives, to multicultural arts and crafts inspired by Bradford's rich mix of religion and race.

All backed up by a hard-working education staff giving interpretations and workshops to help the public get the most out of the gallery.

Open daily, except Mondays, Good Friday, Xmas Day, Boxing Day. 10am - 6pm April to October & 10am — 5pm November to March inc Bank Holiday Mondays.

Lister Park, Manningham Lane, Bradford, Tel 0274 - 493313.

BRADFORD'S INDUSTRIAL MUSEUM is a converted spinning mill with extensive collections, both permanent and changing, of the industrial heritage of Bradford, once "the wool capital of the world."

There are displays of engineering, textiles, working machinery and a local region transport gallery. A millowners and workers houses show domestic life from a century ago.

The smells of lanolin and grease from its working days still pervade the museum and delight the many visitors.

New galleries and exhibits are always being added and the education staff help to bring the past alive in this fascinating building.

Open daily except Mondays, Good Friday, Xmas Day, Boxing Day. 10am — 5pm inc. Bank Holiday Mondays.

Moorside Road, Bradford,
Tel 0274-631756.

City of Bradford Metropolitan Council
Arts, Museums & Libraries
Directorate of Enterprise & Environment

THE MANOR HOUSE, in Castle Yard, Ilkley (tel: 0943 600066). This is a picturesque Elizabethan building that stands on the site of a Roman fort. This C16th and C17th delight houses displays of archaeology, Roman and local history, period room settings and, in the upstairs gallery, a charming exhibition area to showcase local talent.

Ilkley grew to fame in the C19th as a spa resort, and the Manor House displays artefacts and documentation from this period in the town's history. There is also detailed evidence of a Roman fort that stood on the site of the Manor House years ago. The educational value of all this information has not been overlooked, and a lively programme of activities and events is organised by the staff at the museum.

Access to the building is limited for wheelchair users, as even the ground floor is on different levels, and the stairs to the upper gallery are narrow. Museum staff, however, are always available to help visitors with special needs.

THE INDUSTRIAL MUSEUM in Moorside Road, Bradford (tel: 0274 631756). This former spinning mill concentrates on the industrial heritage of the Bradford area. Displays feature engineering, textiles, machine demonstrations and a comprehensive transport collection. The mill owner's house shows domestic life at the turn of the century, and the newly constructed back-to-back cottages highlight the conditions at the other end of the social scale for the mill workers.

Bradford built up its wealth through the textile industry and the floors of looms and machinery suggest the atmosphere of a working mill. The smell of lanolin and grease delight many visitors who once worked in the mills and offer the younger generation an insight into the past. The transport gallery houses a collection of cars built by a Bradford company, Jowett, including the Jupiter sports model which recently ran in the Pirelli Classic marathon.

BOLLING HALL Bowling Hall Road, Bradford (tel: 0274 584140). This is one of the oldest and most interesting houses in Bradford, once the centre of a large estate. The interior reflects the changes from a medieval tower to an C18th wing. The Hall now displays room settings with wonderful period furniture and furnishings, and an important collection of local history material. So close to the city centre yet so far away from the noisy reality of today, Bolling Hall is a true delight.

CARTWRIGHT HALL Lister Park, Bradford (tel: 0274 493313). It was built as a result of the generosity of Samuel Cunliffe Lister, created Lord Masham in 1892. He was the son of a prominent local family and amassed his fortune through the development of new textile technology.

Lord Masham made a major contribution towards the development of the textile industry in Yorkshire, and was one of the people who generated Bradford's enormous late Victorian and Edwardian wealth. In 1870 he sold his family home, Manningham Hall, and the surrounding land to the Bradford Corporation at half the valued price. The land was used to create a public park and Art Gallery and on 4th May 1904 the Prince and Princess of Wales opened Cartwright Hall to an excited public.

The Hall is in the Baroque style first used in C17th Italy. Its most decorative feature is the south facing tower that forms the entrance porch, originally used for guests and civic occasions. It is beautifully decorated with figures expertly carved out of local stone, depicting sculpture and literature, music, drama, architecture and painting. A further four colossal figures surround the tower and these represent important elements of the City's growth and prosperity; spinning, commerce, fortitude, and abundance. There is a sense of light and spaciousness in the building and a never-ending supply of elaborate mouldings and cornices to delight the eye. As the architect Simpson said at the public opening, Cartwright Hall is 'the finest building in Europe of its kind...with the finest carvings in the world.'

The Museum's lively exhibition programme aims to incorporate something for everyone to enjoy, from local art clubs shows to the more academic retrospectives, and all exhibitions are ably backed up by a hard working education staff who provide interpretation and workshops to assist the public to get the most out of the exhibitions. Bradford has a rich cultural mixture of religions and race that add a sparkle to the city's life. This important factor is reflected in the exhibitions and through new purchases for the Museum collections.

The South Pennines authorities, with the wide open spaces available to them, in striving to satisfy the recreational demands of a large local and surrounding population, provide also a great deal of opportunity for outdoor activities for the visitor.

Walking, from brief strolls to the tough miles of the Pennine Way, is catered for everywhere, and pamphlets abound to assist the walker. Those people who like more help, in the form of the security of a guide, will appreciate the many Guided Walks in the area or such Centres as Brownhill (see below), where assistance is offered in walks and more vigorous activities like orienteering.

Pony trekking is also becoming very popular, with stables all over the region catering for beginners as well as experienced riders, and TICs will provide information on local venues for watersports, fishing and golfing enthusiasts.

For the visitor who would like to be outdoors, yet not particularly active, an especial attraction is the **Canal Cruise**. From Shipley and Uppermill, Hebden Bridge and Skipton and many other canal-side towns and villages it is possible to take to the waterways on a variety of trips, from day cruises to brief water-bus rides. This is the leisurely, relaxed, literally laid-back way to see the South Pennines at their most peaceful, sometimes at no more than the gentle pace of a plodding towpath horse.

The trip boat '**Pennine Moonraker**' sails along a restored stretch of the Huddersfield Narrow Canal near Uppermill, within easy reach of the M62 and the Pennine Way. The canal opened in 1811 and was the shortest navigation linking towns on both sides of the Pennines, but included the famous Standedge Tunnel.

Uppermill is the main village of the Saddleworth district of the Pennine foothills and has a local museum and an interesting craft centre. Within a short distance are the attractive villages of Delph and Dobcross, full of quaint tucked-away houses and well worth visiting. Saddleworth is beautifully located, and boasts a particularly fine church which, with two popular inns, is only a mile (1½ km) from Uppermill square. Near Greenfield is the **Dovestones Reservoir**, where waterborne activities take place amid particularly pleasant scenery.

Our Inland Waterways are a haven of peace and tranquillity to be enjoyed by those seeking a rest from noisy, crowded roads. The visitor stepping aboard one of **Apollo Canal Carriers**' passenger cruise vessels is beginning a voyage of discovery - the perfect introduction to the atmosphere and character of the waterways, almost unchanged for two hundred years. Most trips start and finish at Shipley, on the Leeds and Liverpool Canal which provides a water link between east and west coasts.

The Cruise takes passengers from the Wharf Street base, Shipley, back to an age long forgotten, past amazingly varied scenery, through locks and swing bridges and over an aqueduct on the journey to Bingley. The famous 'model village' of Saltaire, and the delightful Hirst Wood are included in this Cruise which turns at the tail of Three Rise Locks in Bingley. Other cruises are sometimes available.

Apollo passenger vessels are an ideal venue for Party Outings, whether it be for a staff outing, wedding reception, company promotion, family celebration, conference or educational trip. Large groups can charter two or even all three vessels, 'Apollo', 'Water Prince' and 'Hebble'. Children's party problems can also be solved by a Party Cruise - Apollo's Party Pack includes food, drink, invitations, balloons and the cruise at an all-in price.

Brownhill Visitor Centre stands at the narrowest point in the valley of the river Tame, a point at which road, canal and railway all run side by side through a gap in the South Pennine Hills - and of course, beneath them all runs the River Tame which goes on to where it once served many of the mills which formed part of Lancashire renowned textile industry.

Any visit to Saddleworth starts at Brownhill Centre. An attractive traditional stone building, it houses exhibitions, which change every 3 months, on aspects of local and national interest. The Tame Valley Warden Service lead guided walks from the Centre, and other activities include river and canal dipping, orienteering, and self guided trails. The Centre provides information on what to see and do in this area of the country, where attractive stone cottages huddle together in steep sided valleys, eyes half shut against winds coming in from the bleak, attractive heather-clad moorlands.

Harewood House is a major attraction in the area (LCC)

Nestling below the Chevin beyond, is the busy market town of Otley in Lower Wharfedale (LCC)

The City of Leeds and its surrounding green countryside have many varied treasures for the visitor to enjoy

Tropical World at Roundhay Park in Leeds offers an unusual alternative for exploration and enjoyment (LCC)

The ruins of Kirkstall Abbey are very impressive indeed in their lovely setting (LCC)

Seen near Hebden Bridge is one of the narrowboats reliving the romance of a bygone era (YHTB)

The picturesque setting of Thornton Viaduct (YHTB)

The rural delights of the South Pennines await our enjoyment and pleasure

Ogden Water is an excellent example of the beauty provided by the many lakes that are found throughout the area (MBC)

Listed below are some of the events which take place around the same period every year. These are as wide ranging as a mud-splattered fell race that has its roots in pre-historic rites, music and dance festivals, carnivals, country fairs, cycle racing and street fairs; and it is all 'serious stuff' with a twinkle in the eye. For South Pennines' **festivals and galas** are an integral part of everyday life. Be it local kids acting out mummers' plays that were first produced in the days of the Crusades, clog-stamping Morris men with a show, the oom-pah-pah of a brass band or some dashing new addition to the annual feasts, festivals and fairs, it is all part of that finest of South Pennines traditions, the love of a 'reet good do'.

This sample is a **random mix** of unmissable oldies and bright new events that cannot, in a short space, do justice to the reality of the jollifications in the South Pennine year. You would be well advised to see them for yourself, which is easy. The difficult part is tearing yourself away afterwards.

ALL YEAR
Throughout the South Pennines there are many guided walks of varying length, various degrees of difficulty and catering for many different interests. Enquire at TICs. In summer there are carnivals and galas galore throughout the South Pennines.

JANUARY
New Year's Day: Rossendale's Hogmanay Hike, an annual walk designed to combat the effects of Christmas over indulgence.
FEBRUARY
Rossendale Way Relay Race, 45 miles (72 kms) cross country around the Rossendale Way.
MARCH
Exhibitions at various venues like the Woodland Heritage Exhibition at the Groundwork Countryside Centre, Rawtenstall. Similar ones, specially for the kids, like Groundwork's Hedgehog Weekend.
APRIL
Rossendale Rossfest at Rossendale.
Burnley National Blues Festival.
Traditional Pace Egg Play along the Calder Valley including Hebden Bridge and Heptonstall.
Coconutters Festival at Bacup where Britain's original urban Morris Dancers don their clogs and dance around the streets and hostelries of the town in what has become a world famous event.
MAY
Cragg Vale Spa Dressing.
May Day events at Piece Hall, Halifax.
Todmorden Carnival.
Holmfirth Folk Festival, which began as recently as 1978 and has been growing in momentum ever since. It has become an annual event held usually during the second week of May and includes Morris, Clog and Longsword dancing, sing-a-rounds and ceilidh, scattered among many venues in the area, including the local pubs.
The annual World Duck Pudding Championships are held in Mytholmroyd where 'Pot Luck' takes on a different meaning throughout the year.
JUNE
Todmorden Agricultural Show.
Harden Moss Sheep Dog Trials take place over a weekend in mid-June on the Association's grounds at Harden Moss on the A635 Greenfield Road. The event always attracts a large and enthusiastic crowd. There is an open sheep dog trial, a sheep dog show and a sheep shearing contest, with side shows, refreshments and a bar.
JULY
Hebden Bridge Old Town Civil War Weekend.
AUGUST
Halifax Show. Halifax Happening, Piece Hall.
Holmfirth Shopping Week is a recently revived event that dates from the 1920s. Each year's festival adopts a particular theme, backed up by a variety of organised events and impromptu performances from street musicians and dancers. Local shops and pubs take up the theme with window displays and fancy dress.
SEPTEMBER
Sowerby Bridge Rushbearing Festival.
Holmfirth Midnight Procession, mid September.
Ilkley Literary Festival, held annually during September, is a week long celebration of books and their authors and attracts book lovers from all over the country with visiting authors, poetry readings, performances, discussion groups, courses, exhibitions, book fairs and the like.
OCTOBER
The annual rally of 7th West Yorkshire Transport Museum, Bradford.
NOVEMBER
Modern traction weekends at the Keighley and Worth Railway.
Bradford Beer Festival, last week in November.
DECEMBER
Halifax Victorian Shopping Days. Piece Hall celebrations for Christmas.

Eight meandering miles (13 kms) northwards from just below Holme Moss, the River Holme flows to join the River Colne at Huddersfield; eight miles of **spectacular scenery** of high hills and broad moorland, of stone-built hamlets, scarcely touched by time, of pleasant woodlands, cared for by the Forestry Commission, of reservoirs, of picnic areas and local pubs that serve good food and good beer. **Holmfirth** is the focal point of the valley; but just see what the rest of it has to offer. It will amaze you, surprise you agreeably, and make you determined to return to places like:-

HOLME This village at the head of the valley nestles under Holme Moss TV mast, which was built in the early 50s, is 221 metres (725 feet) high and was the first TV transmitter for the North of England. The **underground home** of Arthur Quernby is in Holme. Its lawn is its roof! The Fleece is the venue for local foxhounds and beagle hunts.

LONGLEY Its **impressive windmill** is set on a slope above Longley Farm, one of the largest employers in the area. Its dairy products are world renowned.

CARTWORTH MOOR Once wild and disreputable, with cockfighting and a racecourse, and now an area of **lovely walks** through land cleared and planted by the Forestry Commission.

HONLEY An **extremely interesting village** with fascinating shops and alleys. The old wool exchange in Church Street used to be frequented by local people buying and selling wool in the days when cloth was woven at home. The **stocks** are in the churchyard. On one occasion in 1812 Benjamin Walker and Thomas Smith, two Luddites, spent the night drinking at the Coach and Horses, Honley, after having **murdered** William Horsfall, a Marsden mill owner. The landlady was afterwards called to give evidence at the trial in York.

HEPWORTH This settlement suffered from the **plague**, supposedly brought to Foster Place on clothing from London. The infected area was sealed by a barricade near what is now called Barracks Fold. Set in one of the most **dramatic corners** of the valley the village contains many weavers' cottages dating back to the C17th Hepworth Feast, possibly pagan in origin, is held on the last Monday in June.

SCHOLES Roy Castle was born here.

HINCHCLIFFE MILL Just off the main road, here is a mill pond, **beautifully sited** woollen mill and its hillside cluster of weavers' cottages.

WOOLDALE This village contains some of the oldest and most interesting buildings in the district. Its development was greatly influenced by Henry Jackson, a Quaker, and one of the founders of its Friends Meeting House.

NEW MILL Here, in 1780, the first scribbling engine was set up in the Holme Valley, heralding **the Industrial Revolution** in woollen textiles. The hillside around New Mill is riddled with old coal workings and near Meltham House is evidence of an old tramway which took coal from old Bank House Pit to Crowedge Iron and Clay Workings on the other side of the hill.

UPPERTHONG Here the Holm Valley Beagles are kennelled.

HOLMFIRTH This town has had more than its fair share of tears as well as the laughter, for three great floods in 1777, 1852 and 1944 killed nearly a hundred people. Nowadays, though, many visitors coming to Holmfirth are on **a light-hearted pilgrimage** to see the town and countryside inhabited by that lovable rogue Compo, his two faithful companions, Nora Batty with her wrinkled stockings, frustrated Marina and all the other rich characters in the highly successful BBC TV series **'Last of The Summer Wine'**. The homes of Compo and Nora Batty and Sid's Cafe are all in Holmfirth, as is the 'Last of the Summer Wine Exhibition'.

Bamforth comic postcards are an institution. Most seaside holiday resorts stock them because they are designed to make people smile. The **double-entendres** and the outrageous characterisations of portly, overbearing wives and weedy, bespectacled husbands featured on them are hilarious. So if it's laughter you're after visit Holmfirth Postcard Museum.

The Holme Valley really is an agreeable place and, with footpaths kept clear and serviceable by continuous use, this is as good a way as any of exploring the whole of this fascinating part of Kirklees.

The summit of the Calder Valley offers a calm and tranquil landscape for your enjoyment (MBC)

A pretty river scene near the well-known beauty spot of Hardcastle Crags (MBC)

Walking is a very popular pastime in this area - and here at Eaves Wood one can enjoy a tremendous panoramic view (MBC)

The beauties of Calderdale are enjoyed by countless visitors every year

The contrasting colours in the landscape make Brown Hill Reservoir one of the most picturesque spots in the South Pennines (MBC)

The Bronte Parsonage and its museum in Haworth are famous throughout the world for their association with the Bronte Family and their renowned literary works (YHTB)

Of the many interesting historic buildings in Calderdale, these are two excellent places to visit

The appealing architecture and the undoubted wealth of heritage to be experienced in this most attractive of settings makes Shibden Hall near Halifax a must for any visitor (YHTB)

Kirklees Metropolitan District of West Yorkshire calls itself '**Pennine Yorkshire**'. Its south western end is dominated by the vast unspoiled hills of the Peak District National Park - Pennine country - whilst at the other end the towns of **Huddersfield, Batley** and **Dewsbury** spread their influence over the surrounding countryside - and it would be difficult to get more Yorkshire than that!

Between these extremes are the hospitable **valleys of the Colne, Holme and Calder**, with small towns like Marsden, Slaithwaite and Holmfirth, once busy centres of the textile industry but set amidst beautiful countryside and even now appearing to be unsure whether they're rural or urban. **Holmfirth** itself is well worthy of exploration beyond a quick glimpse of scenes familiar from the TV series, and many of the smaller villages show the same signs of having begun as domestic weaving settlements, acquired industrial pretensions, and then lost their way. Netherthong, Upperthong, Underbank and Honley, all in the Holme valley, are examples of **attractive villages** worth exploring for evidence of their textile past. In Kirklees the visitor will be continuously confronted by this confusion of identity, as in the manufacturing mill with its undertones of grime and sweated labour, set upon the scenic hillside alongside its attendant picturesque stone cottages.

Nevertheless, the places where the real brass made its presence felt still burst with Victorian pride in achievement, and the public buildings of **Huddersfield** and **Dewsbury** - whose town centre is a designated Conservation area - are attractive evidence of one of the better sides of the Industrial Revolution. The textile barons of a hundred and more years ago were willing to spend some of their wealth to build corporate celebratory edifices to proclaim to the world both the success of their towns and their own prosperity, and now the reduction of the industry and the cleaning of the air has enabled their buildings to be spruced up and seen again in a condition approaching the splendour of their original state.

The motorways M1 and M62 skirt the northern edges of the Kirklees district, giving easy access from most parts of the country. At a gentler speed, though, it is the narrow winding sideroads which will show the true character of Kirklees, and the towpaths of the **Huddersfield Canals**, the **Kirklees Way**, the **Colne Valley Circular Walk**, or even the rugged miles of the **Pennine Way**, which can best reveal to the visitor the wealth of variety within the Kirklees countryside.

The searcher for **the glories of the past** is well-rewarded in Pennine Yorkshire generally. It is likely that the visitor will be surprised by the number and quality of the old houses and mansions, museums and galleries that abound in the South Pennines as a whole, and Kirklees easily provides its share, with major museums in Huddersfield, Dewsbury and Batley, and smaller ones in Marsden (canals), Golcar (weaving), Holmfirth (postcards, 'Summer Wine'), Overton (mining), and Red House.

Kirklees is also an excellent **centre for touring** further afield. The rest of the South Pennines is easily available to the north and the west - many visitors will appreciate the links through the Brontë sisters between their home in Haworth and several locations in Kirklees. To the north and east lies the broad expanse of Yorkshire and to the south the hills and dales of the Peak and Derbyshire.

The historic city of York, with its famous Minster, Medieval walls and streets, spectacular Jorvik Viking Museum, and Railway Museum, is comfortably within day-visit distance, and even nearer are two of the greatest stately homes in the country. The Duke of Devonshire's beautiful **Chatsworth House**, the 'Palace of the Peak', is in the middle of the Peak District, only 44 miles (70 kms) from Huddersfield, and **Harewood House** is even closer. **The Yorkshire Dales National Park** begins only 38 miles (61 kms) up the road as well... a wealth of days out.

Kirklees may well suffer from a national misconception, that the Yorkshire of the C19th Industrial Revolution in textile manufacturing - the Yorkshire of dark satanic mills, 'muck and brass and nowt else' - still exists unchanged. A first day in Kirklees will be sufficient to show just what has changed, how much it has changed, and how much of the myth never existed in the first place! The towns and villages are different from their industrial days, some very different, but the wide open spaces have always been there, always enjoyed by local people, and now their beauty is accessible to be appreciated by visitors as well.

Inspecting old plans in the underground office or boxhole at the Yorkshire Mining Museum at Overton on the eastern border of Kirklees (YMM)

Kirklees has so much to offer people of all ages

Enjoy the fun of a Victorian Day at Dewsbury Open-Air Market (KMC)

Seen here at Eastergate Bridge at Marsden, these three characters have not only made the whole of Britain aware of the South Pennines, but have also brought a wealth of enjoyment to us in the series 'Last of the Summer Wine' (MH/LSWE)

Farming is an important activity here as elsewhere in the Pennine Hills - and has to force an existence on the very frontiers of economic possibility in the face of Nature's forces (KMC)

The Kirklees region of the South Pennines possesses large expanses of beautiful, unspoilt, open moorland with the varied waterside delights of the green, wooded dales

One aspect of the visual character of the Kirklees and South Pennine landscape is that created by Man in his search for supplies of water for the nearby towns. He has created a vast number of reservoirs that have blended into the natural environment and provided another dimension to its overall beauty (KMC)

For a real taste of the district and face to face contact with the warmth of its people, why not visit one of the wide range of markets in the area? They range from a huddle of stalls in a village to the impressive markets of the larger towns, and a trip to a market will always present the opportunity to do other things as well - Batley, for example, is in an outstanding Conservation Area, and Holmfirth is also set amidst beautiful fringe-of-the-Peak District countryside. Heckmondwike has its Brontë connections, and Cleckheaton is associated with the anti-machinery Luddite insurrections of the C19th. All the towns have buildings worth seeking out, with Huddersfield and Dewsbury being more graced than most.

GENERAL MARKETS Open-air General Markets can be visited at Batley (Fri and Sat), Birstall (Thurs), Cleckheaton (Tues and Sat), Dewsbury (Wed and Sat), Heckmondwike (Tues and Sat), Holmfirth (Thurs), and Huddersfield (Mon, Thurs, Sat). The Huddersfield Market, traditionally referred to, misleadingly, as the 'Monday Market', is partially housed under the cover of a restored Victorian cast-iron structure.

MARKET HALLS These offer the market atmosphere, but under cover, and are open from Monday to Saturday. Huddersfield has the Queensgate Market (½ day Wed), which is a modern building, but Dewsbury's indoor market (½ day Tues) is held in the Victorian Market Hall. Cleckheaton's is known as the Market Arcade (½ day Wed).

SECONDHAND MARKETS this kind of market is a more recent development, and affords the browsing shopper a chance to look over antiques, bric-a-brac and a variety of 'not new' items. In Huddersfield the 'Monday Market' is given over to bric-a-brac on Tuesday, and Dewsbury market takes on a similar guise, 'Going for a Song', on Fridays.

CRAFT MARKETS Craft Markets are another fairly recent addition to the range of markets, as hand-crafted items gain new popularity. Holmfirth Market is devoted to Crafts on a Saturday, and there are craft outlets at Cleckheaton, Heckmondwike and Huddersfield, with Dewsbury joining them in 1991. If what the shopper wants isn't there, many stalls will accept commissions for work to be done to personal specifications.

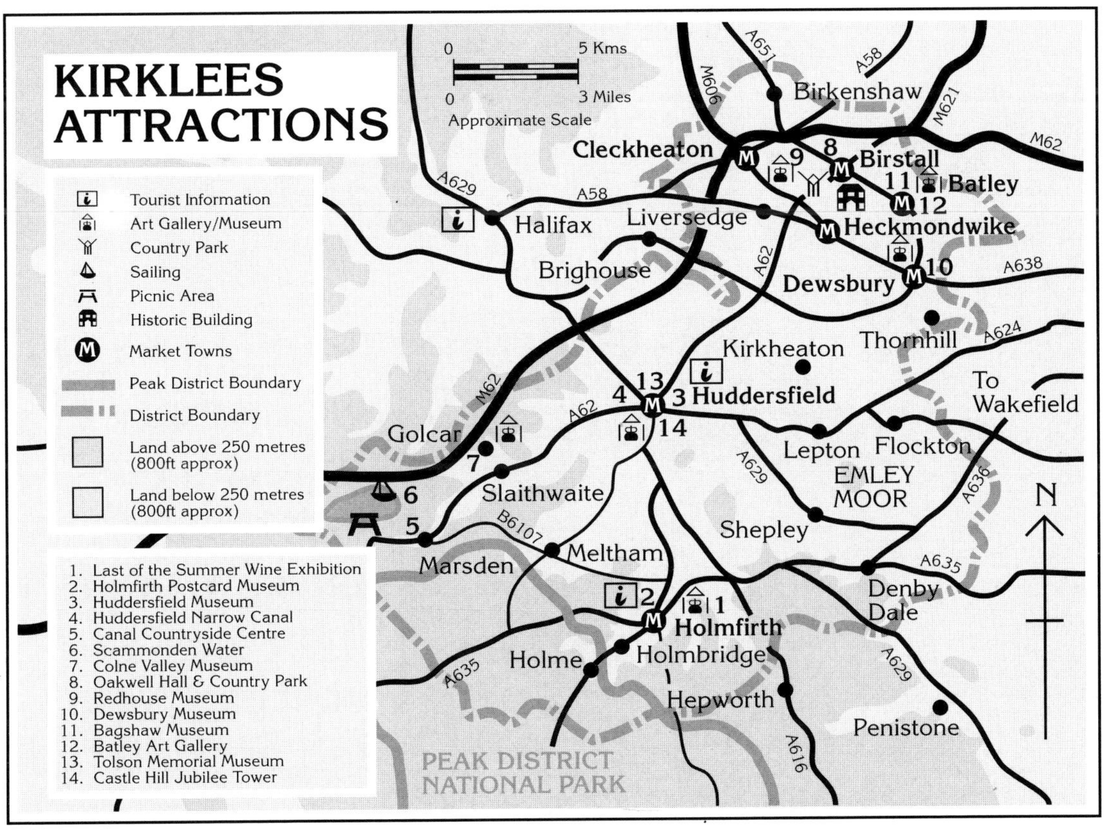

The Bradford Industrial Museum is a most impressive building (BES)

The Bradford area is well-known throughout Britain as the home of the popular television series 'Emmerdale Farm' (BES)

This is just one of the many breath-taking scenes to be experienced at Bradford's National Museum of Photography (NMP)

Bradford has a wide variety of famous and spectacular places to visit and enjoy...... whatever your age and interest

Cartwright Hall in Bradford's Lister Park not only has a most impressive style and setting, but possesses extensive collections of sculptures and paintings (CBMC)

Three of the most interesting historic buildings to visit in the area

Bolling Hall in Bradford is an interesting14th-18th century manor house with collections depicting the social and domestic life of theperiod (CBMC)

The Manor House in Ilkley is an Elizabethan building located on the site of Olicana, the town's old Roman fort......its displays span from its Roman heritage to more recent times (CBMC)

The Standing Conference of South Pennine Authorities, SCOSPA for short, is nothing if not inventive. Take for example, its exciting Trailpass, a super Nature Trail that links nine South Pennine countryside centres, each with a different story to tell.

Trailpasses can be obtained at any of the centres mentioned below and as each one is visited the pass is stamped in the appropriate place. When nine stamps have been collected the pass can be exchanged for a rather super free badge. Visit the centres in any order you choose and if you don't want to sample their mouth watering refreshments or eat your own sandwiches at their picnic areas you don't have to.

There is, of course, a reason for this, a valid reason, not a snag. SCOSPA people are very friendly and like to smile a lot. All, that is, except one, a lugubrious character who shall be nameless. By exploring the centres described on the Trailpass, you will find out about farming conditions in the South Pennines today and yesteryear. So go on, indulge yourself, hit the trail and rest assured that at the end of the trail the person with the widest grin will be yourself.

PENDLE HERITAGE CENTRE Barrowford. A good place for learning about yesteryear farming. There is an old fashioned, C18th barn there, choc-a-bloc with old farming implements, butter churns and tractors. And if that isn't enough for you, test your powers of observation on one of the Barrowford trails. WC including disabled. Refreshments. Tel. (0282) 695366. The shop, tea shop and the Countryside Centre are free but there is a charge for the rest.

TOWNELEY HALL, NATURAL HISTORY CENTRE Burnley. Should you be interested in aquaria, seek no further, for here is shown life in places as diverse as the open sea, inland lakes, fast flowing streams and canals. The grounds are extensive, and include wildlife gardens and a nature trail. Tel. (0282) 24213. Admission to Towneley Hall is free but the main hall is closed on Saturdays. WC including disabled. Picnic area.

BRACKEN HALL COUNTRYSIDE CENTRE Shipley Glen. Budding cordon bleu aspirants can build food chains and make Bronze Age style flour at this centre, which lies between Baildon Moor and beautiful, wooded Shipley Glen. Tel. (0274) 584140. W.C. including disabled.

GROUNDWORK COUNTRYSIDE CENTRE Rawtenstall. Countryside exhibitions and special events are held at this popular rendezvous for countryside enthusiasts. Lots of food and information for digestion and, for a really strange experience, you can walk through a giant willow tree. WC including disabled. Tel. (0706) 211421.

HOLLINGWORTH LANE VISITOR CENTRE Littleborough. Hollingworth Lake is featured in a show about 'Weighvers Seaport'; large fish tanks hold perch, roach and other riverside creatures. They are downstairs, and, by Jove, there could be more wild life upstairs, not to mention what's happening outside. What is happening outside? Come and find out for yourself. WC including disabled. Tel. (0706) 73421.

NORTH DEAN NATURE CENTRE West Vale. Ghost hunters may be unlucky because no one has seen a phantom in this imposing, many-gabled, C17th mansion. People interested in 'hi-tech' displays that explain woodland ecology, however, will have a ball. Some may even remain long enough to be mistaken for ghosts by future visitors. A fascinating 2½ miles trail around North Dean woods begins or ends at the entrance to the Centre, WC including disabled. Tel. (0422) 374014 or 359454.

CHAMBER HOUSE URBAN FARM Heywood. As you explore the fields and the farmyard of this working farm, following an instructive farm trail, it will be seen that everything about it works. Sheep and cows give milk, cockerels crow and hens lay eggs, geese cackle and dogs bark. WC including disabled. Tel. (0706) 48710.

BROWNHILL VISITOR CENTRE Uppermill. Here the upland wildlife displays change with the seasons and, as you would expect, in winter when the surrounding countryside is white, Brownhill is green. Conservation of world wildlife resources is taken seriously here, as it should be everywhere. Tel. (0457) 872598. WC including disabled.

TUNNEL END COUNTRYSIDE CENTRE Marsden. As its name implies Tunnel End is at the end of a tunnel, the longest and highest canal tunnel in Britain. Tunnel End tells the transport story of the Pennines through the ages. WC partial disabled. Tel. (0848) 846062.

.......Don't forget to get your pass stamped.

THE BRONTË WAY From sheltered moorland clough to wild open moorland the Brontë Way offers a glimpse of the landscapes which coloured the imagination of the Brontë sisters. It comprises 9 miles (14½ kms) of strenuous hill walking linking **famous landmarks** including the romantic ruins of Wycoller Hall, Top Withens farmhouse and the Brontë Parsonage Museum.

THE CALDER WAY Take a full week over this one, and it will give you the time to visit nearby places of interest or indulge in a series of day walks using link paths and public transport. **The 50 miles (80 kms) long** Calder Way is both a challenge to the adventurous and an invitation to those with less experience, who can explore the easy stages. The field and woodland paths are now clearly linked to open moor and valley terraces.

THE KIRKLEES WAY What about this! Plague barricades, textile hamlets, knur and spell, Robin Hood's grave, Compo and Nora Batty: What **a glorious mix**! All this is set in the backdrop of wooded valleys, dry stone walls by the mile, moorland and Victorian architectural splendour. If you want some good advice get 'wildly aware' of the Kirklees Way, **a 90 miles (145 kms) long circular walk**, or considerably less if you prefer.

THE PENDLE WAY The Pendle Way is a **45 mile (72 km) walk** around the Borough, split into eight sections, each different in length and character. This produces walking conditions suitable for a range of abilities. The route takes the walker via museums at Pendle Heritage Centre at Barrowford and Bancroft Mill at Barnoldswick to Barley Village and Pendle Hill. In the South Pennines area of the Borough, the Way visits ancient Wycoller, the former Coldwell Inn and reservoirs, and Walverden Reservoir, which provides angling and birdwatching areas. A word of caution: most of today's Pendle Witches are very beautiful and have exquisite figures. Should one kiss you or give you a cuddle you could get turned into a layby!

THE PENNINE WAY On its way from Edale in Derbyshire to Kirk Yetholm in Scotland, the Pennine Way goes northwards from Blackhill right up the middle of the South Pennines to the A59. Within these bounds much is on offer as this **daddy of long distance walks** crosses an exciting Millstone Grit vertebra, first in Lancashire, then Yorkshire, enjoying both, favouring neither: Featherbed Moss with its cotton grass and that sad reminder of the darkest days of industrial depression - the Cotton Famine Road; Black Moss Reservoir; The Ammonn Wrigley Memorial Stone; Trans-Pennine pack horse roads; Blackstone Edge; Stoodley Pike; Heptonstall Moor; Top Withens; Ponder Hall; Lothersdale with its fine working mill water wheel; and Pin Law Beacon. All this and so much more the P.W. provides en passant through the South Pennines; and it can be summed up in just two words, **excitement and challenge**.

ROSSENDALE WAY The Rossendale Way is a circular walk of some **45 miles (72 kms)**, generally across moorland, along the skyline of the Rossendale Valley and dipping down to cross the valleys where necessary. The route has **good links** to the nearby settlements and is described in a series of eight leaflets and a book 'Rossendale Way.'

STANDEDGE WAY Actually it is usually referred to as the Standedge Trail but think of Shakespeare and his roses and the word 'Way' fits equally well. Walk it and you will tread **where the Romans marched** as they passed over the Pennines on their way between Chester and York. Walk it and before long you will be admiring the skills of 'Blind Jack of Knaresborough' in his ability to build turnpike roads. See the 'wonder of the waterways' with its three mile canal tunnel. All these are part of the Standedge Trail, which is a waymarked route across the Pennines between Marsden and Diggle.

THE WORTH WAY From the industrial heart of Keighley walk 5½ miles (9 kms) up the eastern edge of the **Worth Valley to Oxenhope**, through landscape that has changed little since it was described by Mrs. Gaskell when she visited Charlotte Brontë in 1856. From Oxenhope, saunter back through fields past Haworth and Oakworth or go up and over to Top Withens or combine your walks with a ride on the local steam train.

The Keighley and Worth Valley Railway's **beautifully preserved stations** and steam engines are TV and film stars. 'The Adventure of Sherlock Holmes', 'A Woman Of Substance', 'Yanks' and, best known of all, 'The Railway Children', were all filmed here. A special 5 mile (8 km) Railway Children Walk visits many of the memorable and nostalgic locations used during filming.

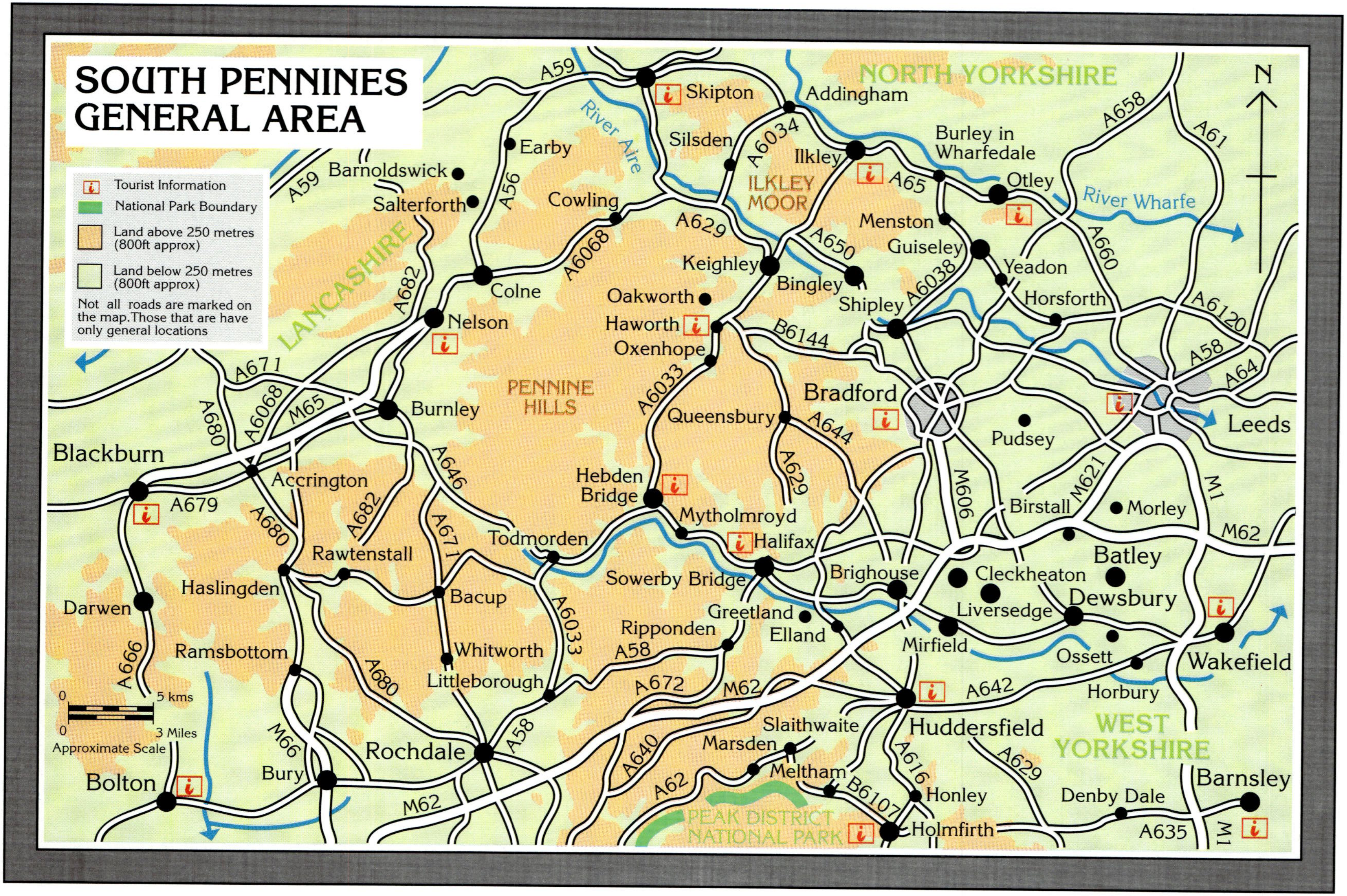
SOUTH PENNINES GENERAL AREA
Tourist Information
National Park Boundary
Land above 250 metres (800ft approx)
Land below 250 metres (800ft approx)
Not all roads are marked on the map. Those that are have only general locations
0 5 kms
0 3 Miles
Approximate Scale
N
NORTH YORKSHIRE
LANCASHIRE
WEST YORKSHIRE
PEAK DISTRICT NATIONAL PARK
PENNINE HILLS
ILKLEY MOOR
River Aire
River Wharfe
Skipton
Addingham
Silsden
Ilkley
Burley in Wharfedale
Otley
Earby
Barnoldswick
Salterforth
Cowling
Menston
Guiseley
Yeadon
Horsforth
Keighley
Bingley
Shipley
Oakworth
Haworth
Oxenhope
Colne
Nelson
Burnley
Blackburn
Accrington
Rawtenstall
Haslingden
Darwen
Ramsbottom
Bolton
Bury
Rochdale
Littleborough
Whitworth
Bacup
Todmorden
Hebden Bridge
Mytholmroyd
Halifax
Sowerby Bridge
Greetland
Elland
Ripponden
Queensbury
Bradford
Pudsey
Leeds
Birstall
Morley
Batley
Brighouse
Cleckheaton
Liversedge
Dewsbury
Mirfield
Ossett
Wakefield
Horbury
Huddersfield
Slaithwaite
Marsden
Meltham
Honley
Holmfirth
Denby Dale
Barnsley
A59
A56
A6034
A65
A658
A61
A629
A650
A6038
A660
A6120
A6068
A682
A671
A6068
M65
A680
A679
A646
A682
A671
A680
A680
A666
M66
A6033
A6033
B6144
A58
A64
A644
A629
M606
M621
M1
M62
A58
A672
A640
M62
A62
B6107
A616
A629
A642
A635
M1
M62
A58

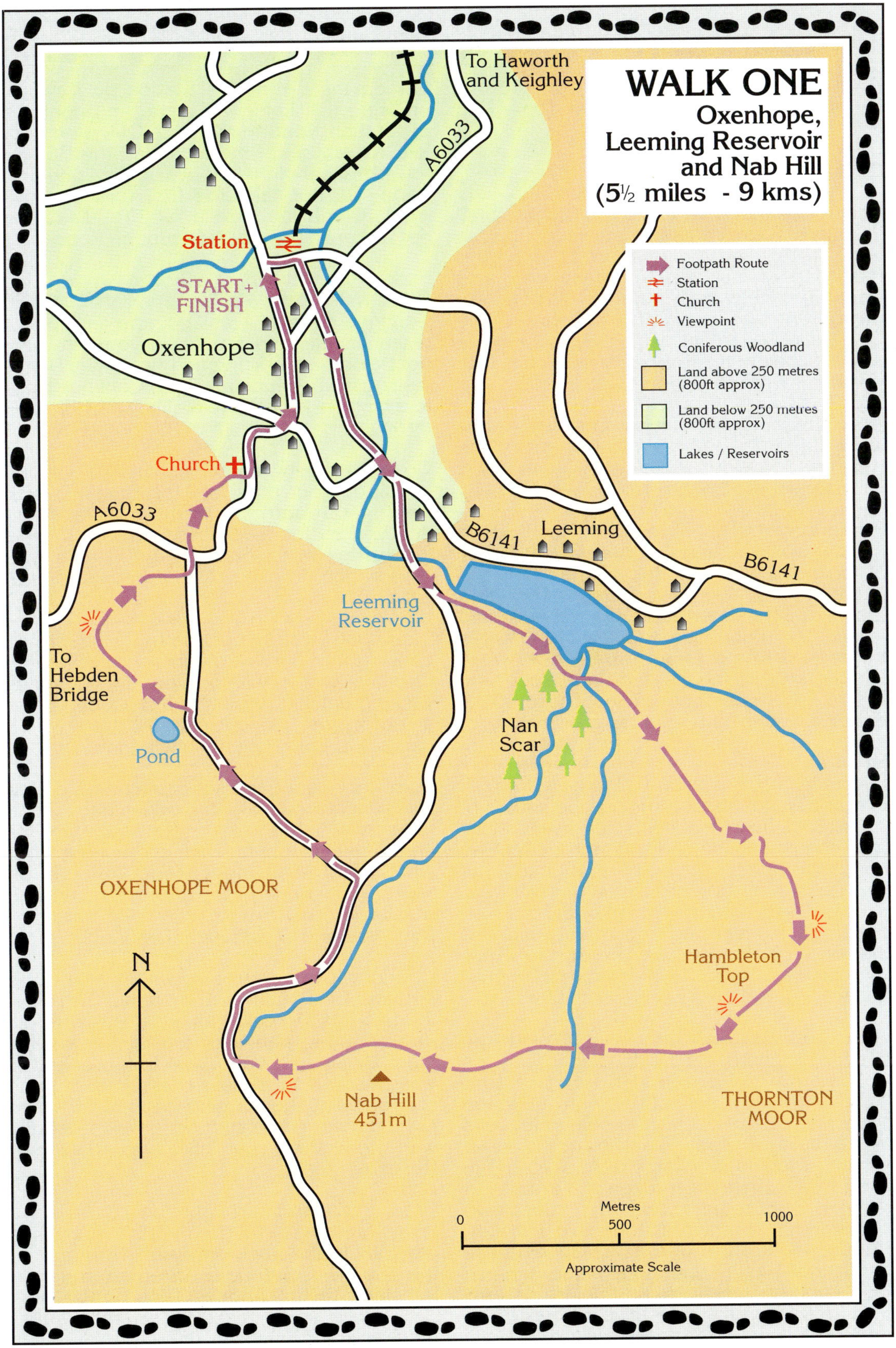
WALK ONE
Oxenhope,
Leeming Reservoir
and Nab Hill
(5½ miles - 9 kms)
Footpath Route
Station
Church
Viewpoint
Coniferous Woodland
Land above 250 metres (800ft approx)
Land below 250 metres (800ft approx)
Lakes / Reservoirs
To Haworth and Keighley
A6033
Station
START+ FINISH
Oxenhope
Church
A6033
B6141
Leeming
B6141
Leeming Reservoir
To Hebden Bridge
Pond
Nan Scar
OXENHOPE MOOR
N
Hambleton Top
Nab Hill 451m
THORNTON MOOR
Metres
0
500
1000
Approximate Scale

Route: Oxenhope - Oxenhope Moor - Leeming Reservoir - Hambleton Top - Nab Hill - Oxenhope

Distance: 5½ miles - 9 kms.

General Description: The water supply to all the large West Yorkshire towns comes, in part, from Leeming Reservoir, Thornton Moor Reservoir, Warley Reservoir and Leeshaw Reservoir, all of which are prominent features along this walk. The Brontës were familiar with Oxenhope Moor as it was before the reservoirs were built. The walking is from moderate to strenuous.

Access: Oxenhope Station, from where this walk starts, is at the southern end of the Keighley and Worth Valley Railway and road links are supplied by the A6033 and B6141.

Route Instructions: Oxenhope Moor, which this fine walk encircles, is home to a variety of moorland birds and this adds interest and excitement to the walk. But this brooding moorland so steeped in drama, romance and legend, has much more to offer. **The Brontës** knew and loved Oxenhope Moor, were familiar with its moods and understood and felt at ease with them. They captured its essence better than anyone else, before or since, in their passionate novels. The Brontës' home at nearby Haworth has become a place of literary pilgrimage from all over the world; and the moors, the source of so much of their inspiration, still sweep away from the parsonage doorway and paths lead out to the Brontës' favourite haunts. It is the Brontë connection that lifts this already excellent walk into the extra special bracket. For to tread where these three very talented sisters trod, to breathe the same sharp moorland air, to savour the same delights is, in a way, like sharing a secret with them.

Although this walk starts at **Oxenhope Station,** its charm can be doubled for anyone able to start at 5 miles (8 kms) distant Keighley, with a delightful steam-powered train ride along the famous **Keighley and Worth Valley Railway**; its ambience of silver screen nostalgia is unforgettable, featured in the 'The Railway Children', 'Yanks', 'A Woman Of Substance' and 'The Adventures Of Sherlock Holmes'. It took two years to build and the line climbs at an average gradient of 1 in 75, through a pleasant, green landscape of steeply sloping fields, streams and dense woodland to its Oxenhope terminus, the real start of the walk.

On leaving Oxenhope Station go forward, crossing Mill Lane with care, and continue up Station Road to the Post Office on your left. Keep going forward, along the B6141, towards Denholme and bear right along **Jew Lane**. Do not take the first fork on your right, which leads to a factory. Take the second one, down a 'No Through Road'.

Follow the track past a house on your left and turn left over a stile immediately after it. Continue close to a wall on your left up to a reservoir. Ignoring a gate on your left, bear right along a track through two gates before leaving it when it bends right. Continue close to a wall on your left to a stile, which you go through.

Go forward between a fence on your left and a wall on your right to a facing stile, which you go through. Go through a door and descend as the wall does. Turn left over a footbridge and continue uphill to a wall corner then down to cross a bridge on your left.

Turn right, upstream, close to the stream on your right to a stile, which you go through. Continue with a wall on your left. Continue walking uphill, crossing two stiles and cross a footbridge. Go up a walled lane which bends left, then right, then left again.

Turn right, along a track, continuing over a stile beside a gate along a walled track. Look for a break in the wall on your right, opposite an old gateway in the wall on your left, over which **Thornton Moor Reservoir** can be seen. Turn right here, along a moorland track. There are fine views of **Leeming Reservoir** and **Oxenhope** on your right.

Continue over a stream, walking with the remains of a wall on your right. Go round the head of the next clough, past some old quarry ruins, and bear left to see **Warley Moor Reservoir**. Walk down to the lane, and walk along it to a radio mast. Pass a pond on your left, then a gate beyond at which turn left over some steps in a wall. Continue with the wall on your left towards **Leeshaw Reservoir** ahead.

Cross a stile and turn right down a track to a lane. Bear left to the A6033. Cross it carefully to the track opposite. Turn right to the church. Continue to the road and bear left back to **Oxenhope.** Turn right at Mill Lane to return to the station; and a super train return to **Keighley.**

Route: Hebden Bridge - Midgehole - New Bridge - Hebden Dale - Gibson Mill - Mytholm - Hebden Bridge

Distance: 6 miles - 10 kms.

General Description: From Hebden Bridge, the unofficial capital of the South Pennines, this walk meanders very pleasantly along two delightful, wooded valleys, the path, for much of the way, following the course of Hebden Water. The common land the walk crosses, midway along it, adds contrast; an early C16th pack horse bridge and Nutclough Mill, which was a highly successful co-operative mill between 1873 and 1919, give a soupcon of history. The walk encounters an oddity almost at the start. St. George's Square in Hebden Bridge is not a square at all - it is a triangle. In it, every Good Friday, mummers perform a traditional Pace Egg Play in which 'Good', represented by King George, triumphs over 'Evil', the Black Prince.

Access: There is a car park near the Tourist Information Centre, Hebden Bridge, on the A646, from where the walk starts. Bus stops are nearby and frequent train services from Leeds, Manchester and Preston.

Route Instructions: From the rear of the car park beside the Information Centre in **Hebden Bridge** go upstream along a riverside path, cross the pack horse bridge and shortly turn right into Hangingroyd Lane. The pack horse bridge, which replaced an earlier wooden bridge, dates from the early C16th.

At the end of the lane turn right, then left to re-cross the river and go along the lane on your left, past some swings. Soon after the lane veers right, take the path to the left leading to a foot-bridge, which you cross. Now cross the stile beyond it, climb the steep lane ahead to a junction and turn right along a lane past some houses. Continue along the woodland path ahead and bear right, downhill, where it bifurcates. On reaching a track coming from the bowling green bear left along it. Where it bifurcates bear left again and continue, climbing gradually.

Pass a farmhouse on your right and continue along a walled lane above it for 100 metres, turn sharp left and then right to climb a stone stair case, which leads to a lane. Turn right here, passing some trees on your left and after 200 metres bear right along the route of the **Calderdale Way** along a lane that leads to **New Bridge.** Cross the bridge on your right.

Turn left down the steps at a National Trust sign and continue along a wooded path upstream to **Gibson Mill** with the river on your left.

Gibson Mill was founded by Abraham Gibson around 1800 as a water powered cotton spinning mill. Its chimney was added when steam power was introduced in the 1860s, thus solving the problem of water in dry, frosty weather. Children aged from 10 to 12 were employed there, working a 72 hour week for half a crown. It closed in the 1890s because of competition from Calderdale's larger and less remote mills.

Cross the river on the bridge near Gibson Mill, turn left along a lane to reach a sharp bend where you go straight ahead, up some steps, to a gate into a field. Continue straight ahead to a road and turn left to reach a walled track on your right. Go along the track, pass a farm, and on reaching a common, cross it, close to a boundary wall on your right, and on reaching a wood turn right along it.

Before reaching a row of cottages turn left and descend into a farmyard. Turn right through a narrow opening between two barns and go forward crossing three stiles, before turning left, downhill, with a wall on your left. Near the bottom of the field bear right to a stile in the bottom wall, which you go through. Cross the corner of the next field. exiting at another stile. Descend to cross another stile and turn left along the **Calderdale Way,** paved at this point, with a wall on your left. Cross a stile into a wood then go left across a waymarked stile along a paved path. Cross a stile in the far left of the field ahead. Pass a gate on your right and turn right over a stile to go along a paved path.

After crossing several stiled fields, the path joins a track. Bear left along this track and, where it bifurcates, go right. Pass some cottages and cross a stile to follow a paved path to another stile. Continue from here along a clear track and take the right fork down hill to a lane. Cross it and continue downhill close to a wall on your right. Turn sharply right at a road and then left.

Cross a bridge and bear left along **Eaves Road.** Pass St. James' Church and go along Church Lane to the A646, where go left, along it back to the start of the walk.

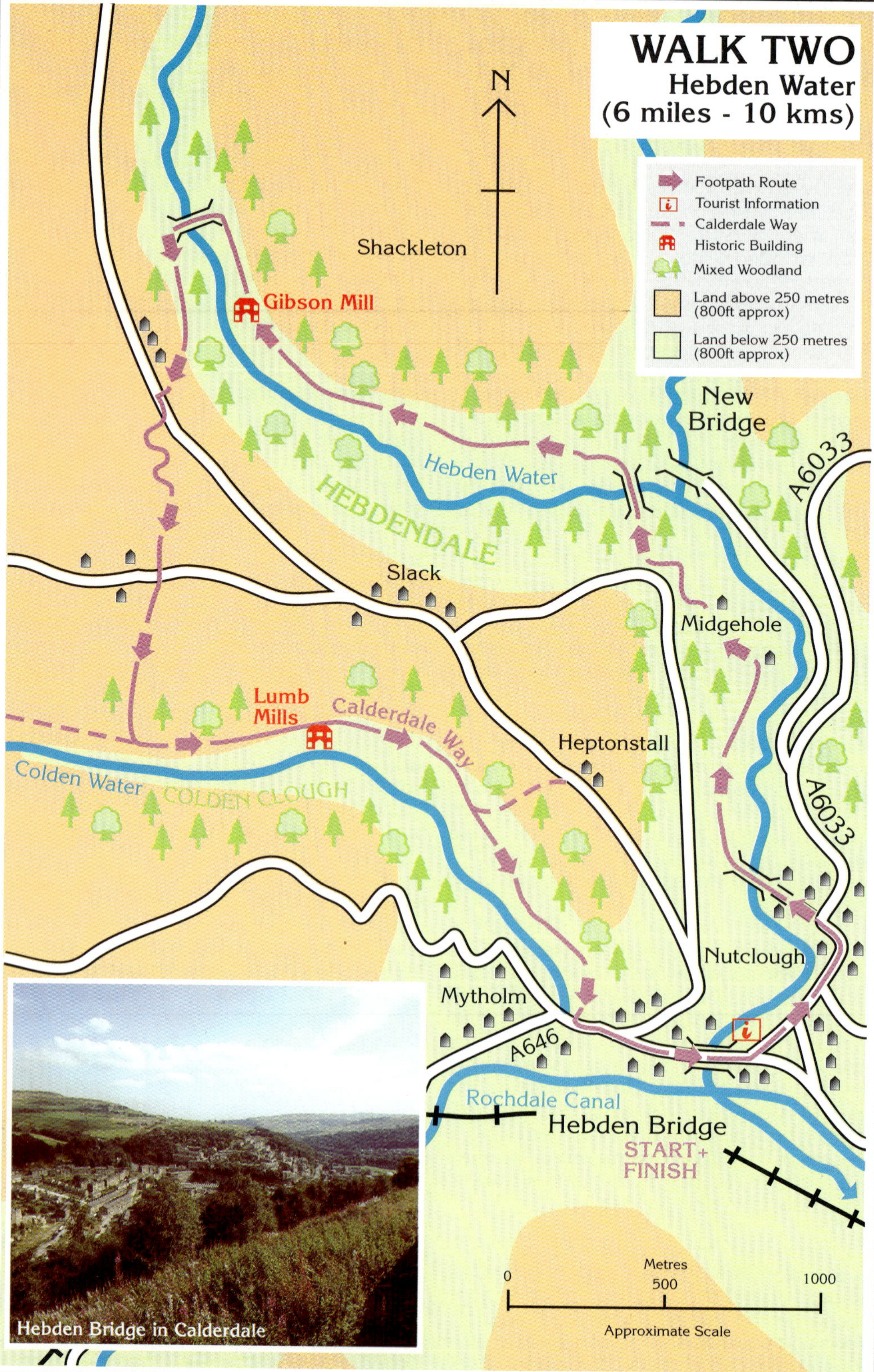

Hebden Bridge in Calderdale

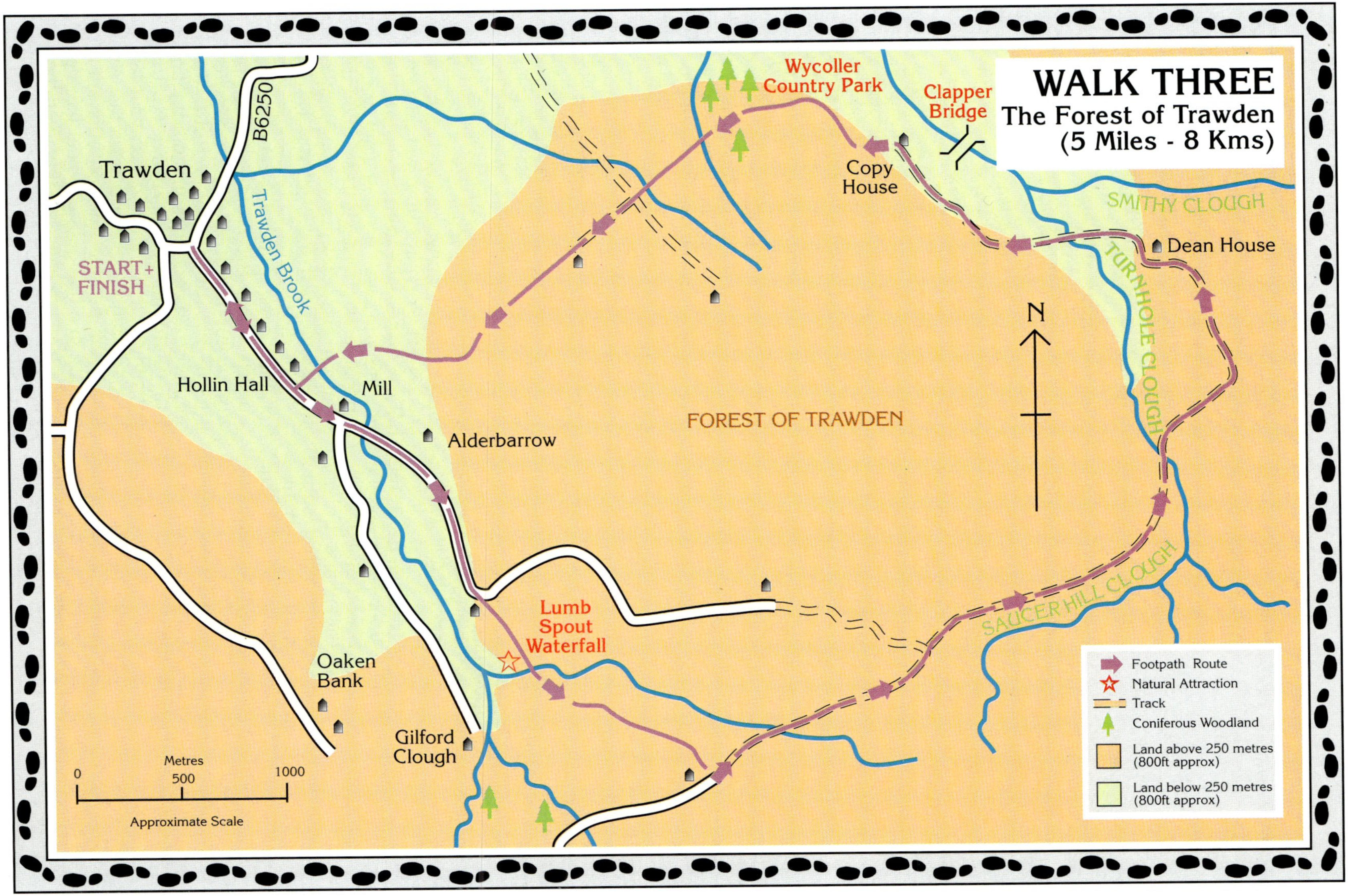
WALK THREE
The Forest of Trawden
(5 Miles - 8 Kms)
Wycoller Country Park
Clapper Bridge
Copy House
SMITHY CLOUGH
Dean House
TURNHOLE CLOUGH
Trawden
B6250
Trawden Brook
START + FINISH
Hollin Hall
Mill
Alderbarrow
FOREST OF TRAWDEN
N
SAUCER HILL CLOUGH
Lumb Spout Waterfall
Oaken Bank
Gilford Clough
Metres
0
500
1000
Approximate Scale
Footpath Route
Natural Attraction
Track
Coniferous Woodland
Land above 250 metres (800ft approx)
Land below 250 metres (800ft approx)

Route: Trawden - Hollin Hall - Dean House - Saucer Hill Clough - Bank House - Copy House - Trawden

Distance: 5 miles - 8 kms.

General Description: The walking is moderate and the route is across rich, peaty moorland. Lumb Spout, passed on the outward leg about ½ mile beyond Hollin Mill, is a fine waterfall, especially after a period of wet weather. The moorland on Boulsworth Hill, on the south side of Saucer Hill Clough, has been designated as a Site of Special Scientific Interest. Heather, bilberry and cloudberry grow there and it is home to linnet, redshank, skylark and snipe. Part of the route coincides with the Pendle Way and is identified by 'witch' waymarkers. The looming bulk of Pendle broods to westward and the Pendle Way, even in these unbelieving times, remains magical, mysterious and stained with dark associations. See the chapter 'The Pendle Witches'.

Access: The bus terminus at Trawden, from where the walk starts, is served by buses from Nelson and Burnley.

Route Instructions: At one time there were trees in the Forest of Trawden; but not any more. Rich peat soil testifies to their former presence. It was a hunting ground for Saxons and eventually, gradually, the trees were felled for farmland. Lime was added to the soil to improve it and stone walls were built to enclose it. The route of this walk is across unimproved moorland which rises to form Boulsworth Hill to the South of Pendle Way.

From the bus terminus in **Trawden** go up the lane to pass the mill on your left. Continue over a bridge and onto a bend on your left, where leave the lane and continue straight ahead along a farm track. Go past some farm buildings on your right and continue through a gate. Go ahead with a wall on your right and through a second gate. Continue ahead along a track to cross a beck where a diversion to the right to see **Lumb Spout** waterfall is recommended. Lumb Spout is a splendid sight in wet weather.

On returning to the bridge veer left, uphill, as directed by a waymarker post. Cross a stile beside a gate in a wall corner and continue with a wall on your right. Cross a ladder stile and turn left along a track with a wall now on your left. This is part of the **Pendle Way,** so follow the 'witch' waymarkers. The path goes above a stream on your right; eventually to descend to cross this stream as indicated by a waymarker. Now bear left to cross a stile beside a gate.

Continue along a track with a wall on your right. As the field narrows, look for a signpost ladder stile beside a gate on your left and turn left over it. Continue along a fence, then a wall, on your left to a stile near a gate, which cross. Bear left to pass **Dean House** on your right, then go left, over a stile in a wall and bear right to cross another stile in a fence in front of a stream.

Cross the stream and go over the stile in the fence on its far side. Bear right, uphill, by a waymarker post. Turn right, through a stile near the top of the wall on your right and continue to a stile on your left. Cross the stile in the wall on your left at **Bank House** and turn right as waymarked to go through a gate. Follow the track above a wall on your right. Soon some trees behind a fence on your left are passed. Continue over a stile in a corner and go forward beside a wall on your right for 30 metres. Turn right to cross the wall and reach the corner of a field on the other side.

Bear left towards **Copy House** and along a path between a fenced plantation on your left and a wall on your right. Go through a gate towards the house and turn left up a waymarked path to the top gate. Bear right along a path which climbs gradually to cross a stile beside a gate. bear right along a surfaced track and when level with a wall on your left look for a waymarked path and turn sharply left along it with a wall now on your right. Cross a stile, with trees now on your left, when the wall on your right goes right, continue ahead through trees. Soon there is a wall on your left. Cross a stile in the corner and go ahead with a wall on your left.

Continue over a stile keeping the wall on your left. Cross two more stiles and pass a farmhouse on your left before going over a stile in the corner of a field. Pass a farmhouse on your right and turn right over a stile beside a gate. Turn left along a waymarked path with a wall on your left. Go ahead, through a stile and down the left side of the field; passing trees on your left. Turn left through a tiny gate and bear left, down a track. Cross a bridge over a beck to the right of the mill. Turn right along the lane, back to the bus terminus.

Route: Marsden to Menston

Distance: 59 miles - 9½ kms

Access: There are railway stations at each end of this spectacular, sometimes strenuous cycle tour.

Route Instructions: The route directions are given northwards from Marsden. Should you be in trouble keep on a major road. If given no directions to the contrary, keep straight ahead.

From **Marsden Parish Church** go to the junction of Station Road and the Green where go right to the Swan Public House. Continue straight ahead past the United Church, ignoring a wider road which bears right. In one mile go under a railway bridge then immediately left into a narrow surfaced road, uphill. In one mile turn left at the Rose and Crown. Follow a surfaced road for 2½ miles (4 kms). Turn left at a T-junction, then bear left after 250 metres to the A640 and stay on it to Buckstone's Junction.

For a scenic route round **Scammonden Water,** turn first right on the A640 onto O'Cot Lane to a major car park. Then go left on a road round the head of the reservoir which rejoins the main route.

At Buckstones turn back right along the A6025 - cross the M62 to **Ringstone Reservoir.** Turn back, left alongside the reservoir and continue for 1¾ miles (3 kms) to a picnic site at **Booth Wood Reservoir.** Take the A672 to the Turnpike Inn and turn right into Pike End Road. Shortly, turn left at a T-junction and continue for 1¾ miles (3 kms) to Baitings Reservoir and the A58, where you turn left for 100 metres, then right into Blue Bell Road. At the Blue Bell Inn, fork left and soon fork left again. For the next 4 miles (6½ kms)continue to fork left whenever the surfaced road divides. Turn left at the Shepherd's Rest in **Hubberton**, left at a T-junction, then right in 250 metres at the next cross roads past Lane Ends House. Go forward for just over a mile to reach a 'No Through Road' sign. Turn right at a T-junction, then left onto Scout road for a mile to **Mytholmroyd**. Turn right at a T-junction signposted Hebden Bridge. Go left onto the A646 at Dusty Miller and on to **Hebden Bridge.**

From the Hebden Bridge Tourist Information Centre near the traffic lights, cross the frontage of Bridge Gate car park. Turn right into St. George's Square, bear left, then cross the A6033 and continue obliquely left, uphill, passing Stubbin's School. Pass Birchcliffe Centre on the left, then go immediately left signposted 'Link Path to Calderdale Way'. Go half right at the top of the slope then left in 100 metres by a bungalow. Then turn right at the Hare And Hounds. In 2¾ miles (4½ kms) bear left at the Sportsman Inn, **Midgley.** Fork right after High House when faced with a 'No Through Road' road sign, then back, right, at the next bend. On the outskirts of Booth Village turn sharp left. Shortly, turn right at a T-junction. Go left at the Cross Roads Inn. Fork right on approaching Wainstalls. Continue on the road over the moor, part of which is unsurfaced, for 3 miles (5 kms) to a T-junction with the A6033 and go right to **Oxenhope.** Turn left at the crossroads and right just beyond the station. Go right at a T-junction and continue for 1¾ miles to **Haworth.** Go left at a T-Junction in Haworth, up the cobbled main street. Bear left by the Tourist Information Centre and then left again. Fork right by de-restriction signs. Continue through **Stanbury** and past **Ponden Reservoir.** Turn back, right, at the first junction after the reservoir and continue for 3½ miles (5½ kms) to **Oakworth.** Bear left at the Golden Fleece. Go left at a T-junction. Bear left at the top of the slope and left at the cemetery. After 2¼ miles (4 kms) go right into Coppy Lane. In 2 miles (3 kms) turn right into **Laycock.** Go left at the Methodist Church and right at a T-junction. Continue to **Redcar Town** and left to **Steeton.** On approaching Steeton centre turn left after a wall post box to the A629, then right to the traffic lights.

From the junction of the A629, and the A6034 go along the A6034 to **Silsden.** Cross the canal and in 40 metres turn right. Turn left at the cemetery into Hawber Lane, signposted to Ilkley, and take the first right into Brunthwaite Lane. In 2¾ miles (4 ½ kms) turn right and after 3 miles (5 kms) fork right. At the A65 turn right towards **Ilkley.** On approaching the town turn right soon after some 40mph signs into Victoria Avenue. Turn left at a pillar box into Grove Road, which is unsigned, continue forward through the town, pass the station and fork right, signposted Cow and Calf Rocks for 3¼ miles (5 kms) to **Burley Woodhead**.

Continue for a further mile and go left towards **Menston,** where this stretch ends at Menston Recreation Ground.

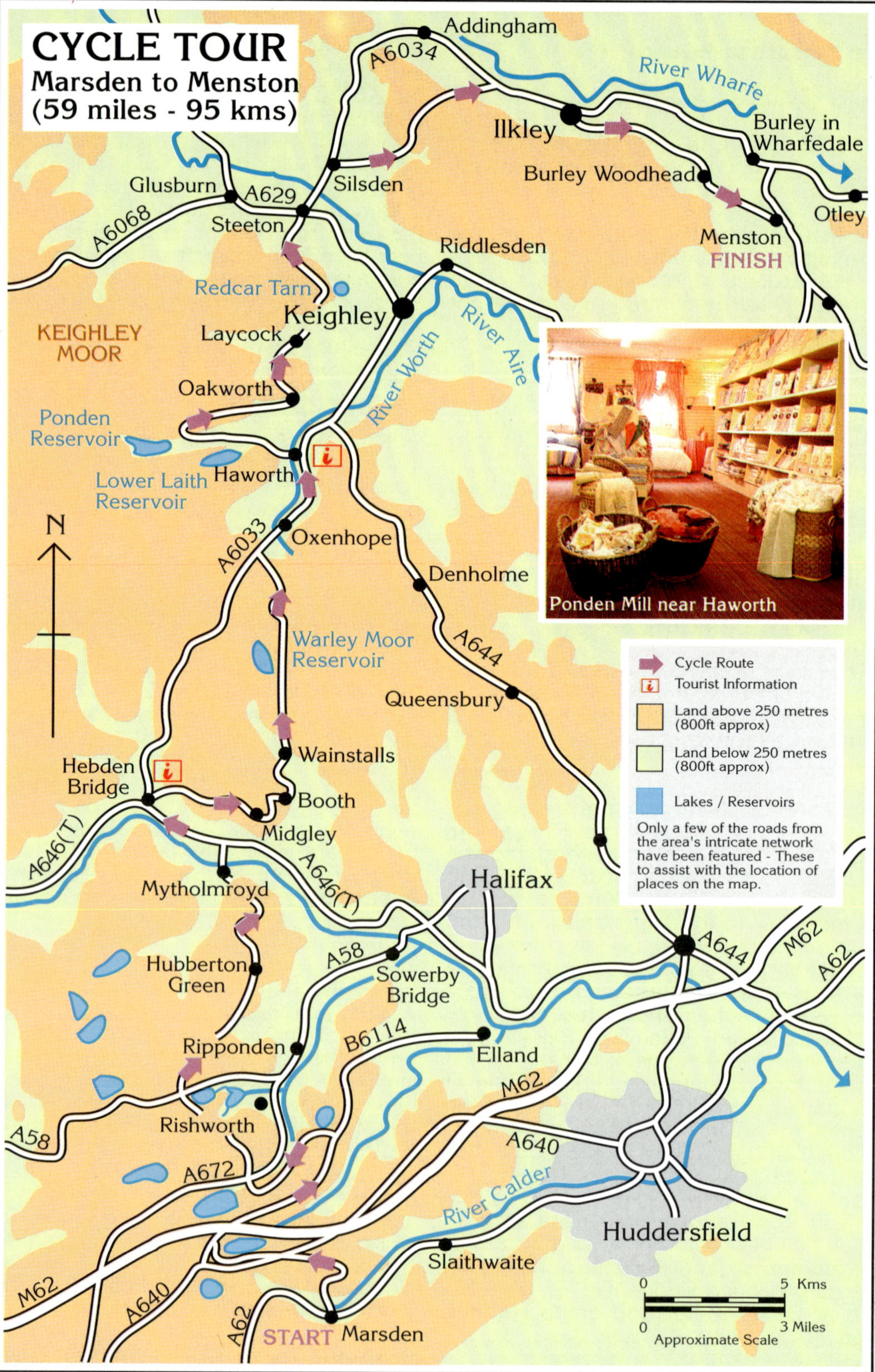

CYCLE TOUR
Marsden to Menston
(59 miles - 95 kms)
Addingham
A6034
River Wharfe
Ilkley
Burley in Wharfedale
Burley Woodhead
Otley
Menston
FINISH
Silsden
Glusburn
A629
A6068
Steeton
Riddlesden
Redcar Tarn
Keighley
River Aire
River Worth
KEIGHLEY MOOR
Laycock
Oakworth
Ponden Reservoir
Lower Laith Reservoir
Haworth
N
A6033
Oxenhope
Denholme
Ponden Mill near Haworth
Warley Moor Reservoir
A644
Queensbury
Cycle Route
Tourist Information
Land above 250 metres (800ft approx)
Land below 250 metres (800ft approx)
Lakes / Reservoirs
Only a few of the roads from the area's intricate network have been featured - These to assist with the location of places on the map.
Wainstalls
Hebden Bridge
Booth
Midgley
A646(T)
Mytholmroyd
Halifax
A644
M62
A62
A58
Hubberton Green
Sowerby Bridge
B6114
Ripponden
Elland
Rishworth
M62
A640
A58
A672
River Calder
Huddersfield
Slaithwaite
0 5 Kms
0 3 Miles
Approximate Scale
M62
A640
A62
START
Marsden

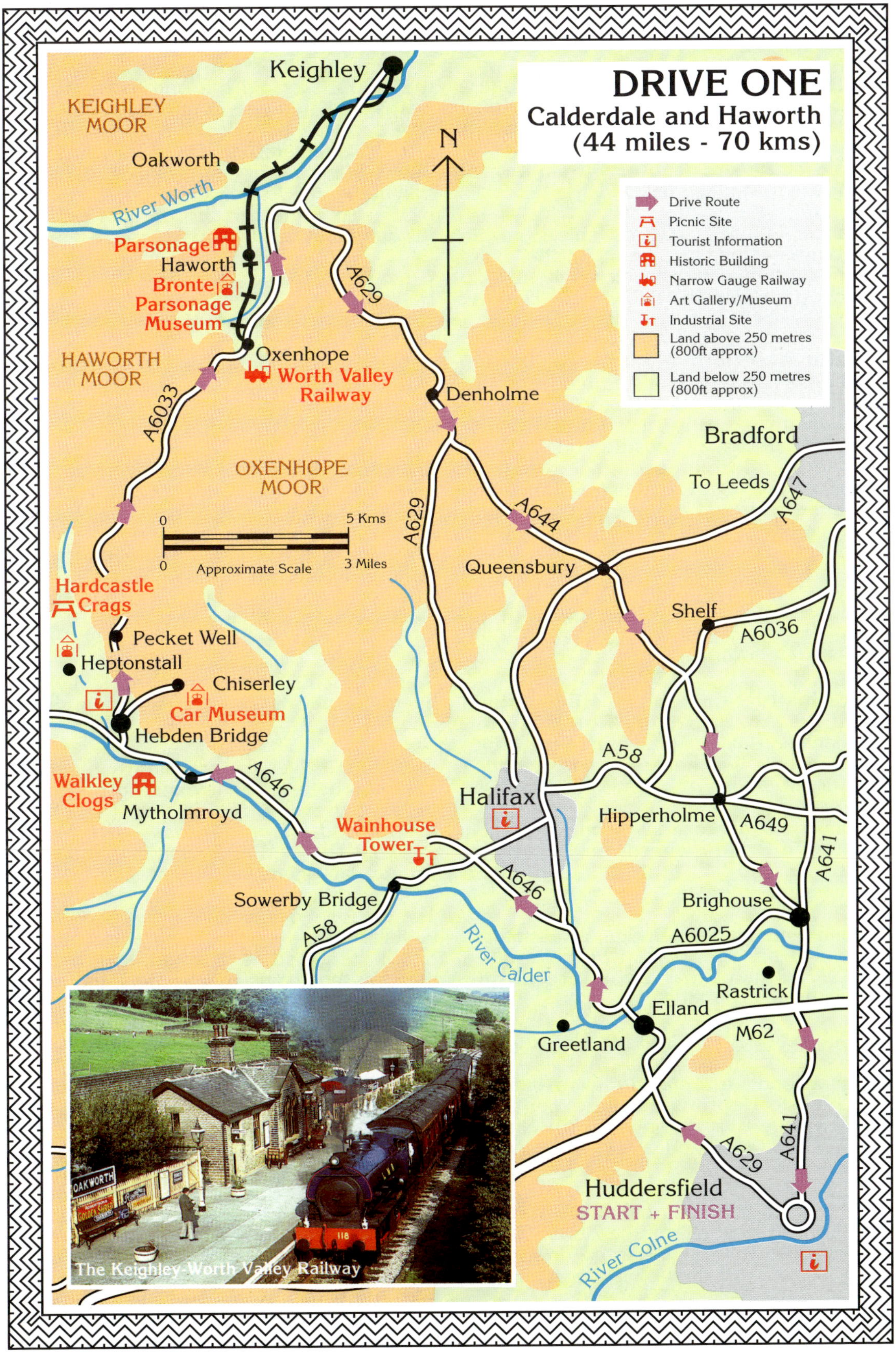

The Keighley-Worth Valley Railway

Route: Huddersfield - Hebden Bridge - Heptonstall - Hardcastle Crags - Hebden Bridge - Brontë Moors - Oxenhope -Haworth

Choice of Return Route: via Halifax or Brighouse to Huddersfield.

Distance: 44 miles - 70 kms. This is only an approximate measurement, as the exact distance will depend on which diversions, if any, you choose to follow from Hebden Bridge (see below).

General Description: All that is best in Calderdale and Haworth is embraced in this delightful drive across the brooding Brontë moors with exciting diversions to visit splendid Hardcastle Crags and other places of diverse and exceptional interest. A suggested break at Oxenhope will give you a chance to travel on the famous Worth Valley Railway. For Brontë lovers this is a must.

Access: This drive starts at Huddersfield which is fed, clockwise from the north, by the A641, A62, A642, A629, A616, A6024, B6108, A62, A640, and A629.

Route Instructions: Leave **Huddersfield** along the A629, Halifax Road, and on approaching Halifax turn left onto the A646. After one mile **Wainhouse Tower** is reached on your left.

Continue until approximately one mile short of Hebden Bridge where, on the left, is **Walkley's Clog Factory**, the only one surviving in Britain.

Continue into **Hebden Bridge**, a fascinating town and an important South Pennine centre from where **two interesting diversions** can be made.

For the first one leave Hebden Bridge going westwards along the A646, then follow clear signs around, 'turning circle' to climb a steep hill to **Heptonstall**, an exceptional hilltop village with a ruined C13th church, weavers' cottages and a C17th Grammar School.

For the second one go north in the Haworth direction and turn left, off the A6033, into a deep wooded valley, substantially owned by the National Trust, and continue along it to Hardcastle Crags.

The main route leaves Hebden Bridge along the A6033, as did the one to Hardcastle Crags, but this one continues northwards where, a little beyond the Hardcastle Crags turn off, an interesting diversion right to **Old Town, Wadsworth**, can be made to visit, in Billy Lane, the **Automobilia Car Museum** or indulge in a meal in **the Berghof** Austrian restaurant, at nearby Crossstone.

Continue along the A6033 towards Haworth. This is the scenic route over the Brontë Moors and the road divides Haworth Moor and Oxenhope Moor. This is a particularly dramatic section of this route and it offers fine views in all directions. The road descends into Oxenhope at the southern end of the Worth Valley.

Oxenhope is an ideal mid-drive stop for it gives you a rare chance to have a relaxing trip on a **Keighley and Worth Valley Railway** steam train, an opportunity to go back in time along the steam railway that found fame in the film of 'The Railway Children'. The small railway museum at Oxenhope Station is well worth a visit.

The A6033 skirts **Haworth** and parking there can cause problems. Yet, really, this internationally famous, Brontë village should not be missed.

Oxenhope solves the problem by offering a convenient and most exciting means of getting there, travelling on the above mentioned Keighley and Worth Valley Railway. The journey is a short one and the **Brontë Parsonage Museum** awaits.

The Parsonage was the former home of the novelist sisters Emily, Anne and Charlotte and is furnished as it would have been in their day, including manuscripts and family possessions. The Parish Church and the Black Bull Hotel also have important links with the Brontë family.

From Oxenhope continue northwards along the A6033 to Cross Roads where the A629 is joined.

Go right, along it almost to **Denholme Clough** where the road bifurcates and a choice of return routes is offered. Either fork right along the A629 and return to **Huddersfield** by way of Halifax or go left along the A644 to Brighouse, where you take the A641 to Huddersfield. Whichever route you choose will bring you to the end of a most enjoyable drive.

Route: Huddersfield - Holmfirth - Uppermill - Dobcross - Delph - Marsden - Golcar - Milnsbridge - Huddersfield

Distance: 38 miles - 61 kms.

General Description: Saucy postcards, Sid's Cafe and Nora Batty's house, the lovely Pennine slopes where Compo and his memorable companions played out their hilarious adventures, canal scenery, weavers' cottages, railway tunnel vents, lonely moors and bustling little Pennine towns together form an integral part of this super drive's fabric.

Although not especially long, this drive passes many very interesting places, such as the Brownhill Visitor Centre or the Colne Valley Museum, at which you may well wish to spend some time. You should therefore allow a day for the drive and will then have the time to enjoy the many delights it offers.

Access: This drive starts at Huddersfield which is fed, clockwise from the north, by the A641, A62, A642, A629, A616, A6024, B6108, A62, A640 and A629.

Route Instructions: Leave **Huddersfield** along the A616, branching right at Honley along the A6024 to **Holmfirth** at the very heart of 'The Last of the Summer Wine' country.

No introductions should be necessary to this popular tour stop. Explore setted ginnels around the Church and the river. Find Nora Batty's house and you may find them filming.

There is a good range of shops including the gallery of television's favourite water-colour artist, Ashley Jackson, the famous **Postcard Museum, the 'Last of the Summer Wine' Exhibition** and the Saturday craft market that adds greatly to the town's atmosphere.

Continue along the A635, Manchester road, which, for a little way, cuts into the **Peak District National Park**. The drive is a very scenic one over some of England's most dramatic landscape. There is a picnic area, Binn Green, above Dove Stone Reservoir on the west side of the Pennines.

Now follow the A669, Oldham road, and the A670 into **Uppermill,** a bustling, small, Pennine town through which runs the historic Huddersfield Narrow Canal. Other attractions include an Art Gallery and Saddleworth Museum.

Leave Uppermill along the A670 and after half a mile (1 km) go left, along the A6052 to reach the **Brownhill Visitor Centre** which houses changing exhibitions on countryside matters. There are various opportunities here for the more energetic to get involved in some outdoor, sporting activity.

Returning to the A670, continue along it for 2 miles (3 kms), passing the Navigation Pub on your left and turn left into **Dobcross.** Drive through the village, one of the most attractive in the Pennines. On reaching the A6052 turn right, into **Delph**, crossing the junction with the A62.

Delph is an attractive weavers' village beside the River Tame and has various gift shops and a riverside walk.

Return to the junction with the A62 and continue in the direction of Huddersfield. This is a **scenic route** across which the Pennine Way passes on a footbridge. From it are seen railway tunnel vents, Britain's longest canal tunnel under **Standedge** and 'Blind Jack' of Knaresborough's famous turnpike road.

Continue past the Pennine mill towns of **Marsden and Slaithwaite**. On reaching Milnsbridge follow the signs to **Golcar** along the B6222, where is to be found the **Colne Valley Museum.**

Return to the A62 and continue along it to **Huddersfield.** Alternatively, instead of passing Marsden, turn off the A62 into Station Road, **Marsden** and follow the road through the village, over the canal and railway bridge.

Turn left into Reddisher Road and continue to the **Tunnel End Canal and Countryside Centre**, turning left at the Junction Public House.

Coaches are not able to turn here but must continue along the road to Hey Green, a hotel and restaurant.

Tunnel End Canal and Countryside Centre is a former tunnel keeper's cottage and is sited beside the longest canal on the highest section of canal in the country. Return to the A62 and continue along it via Milnsbridge back to **Huddersfield.**

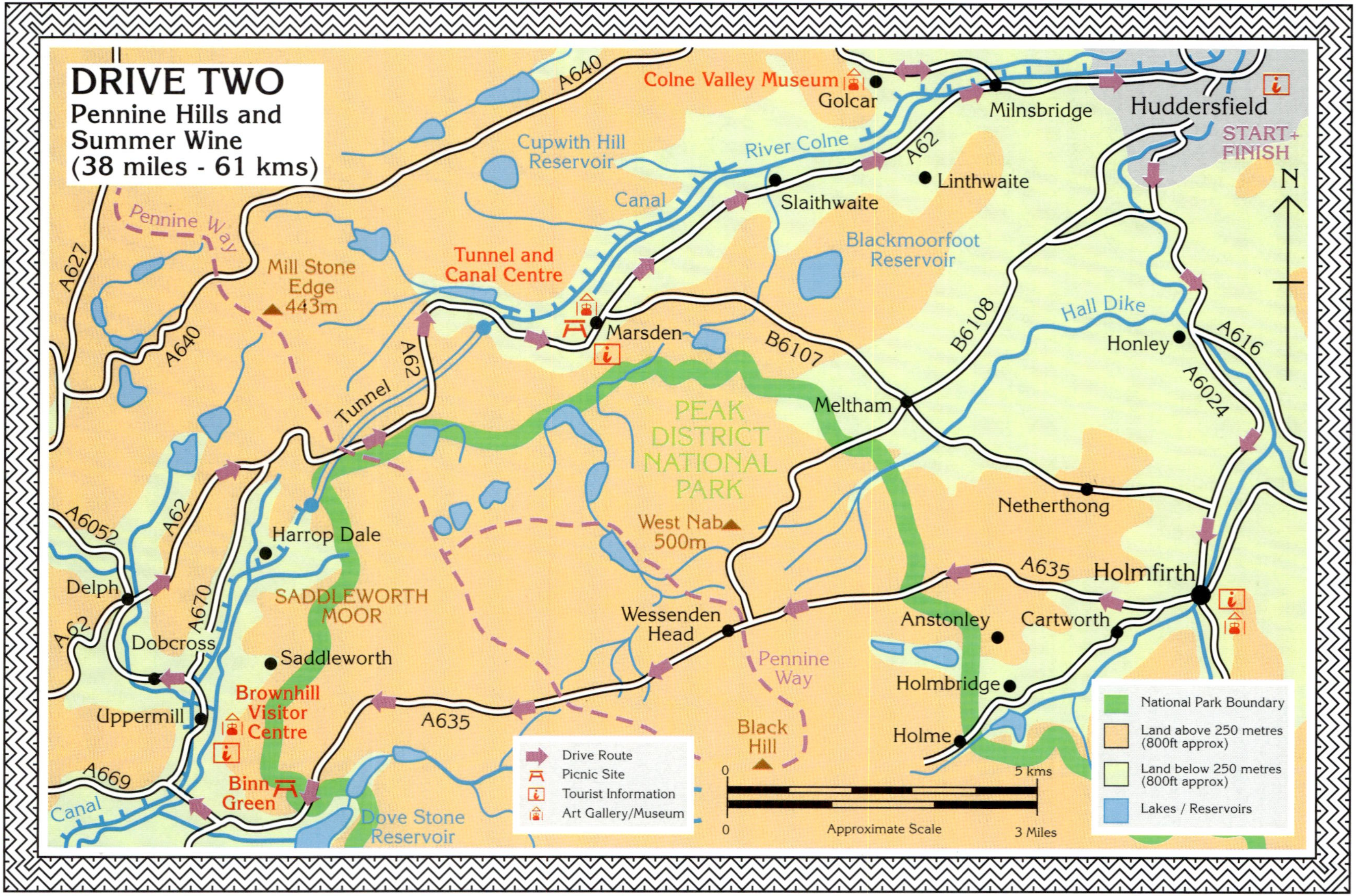
DRIVE TWO
Pennine Hills and Summer Wine
(38 miles - 61 kms)
Colne Valley Museum
Golcar
Milnsbridge
Huddersfield
START+ FINISH
N
Cupwith Hill Reservoir
River Colne
Canal
A62
Linthwaite
Slaithwaite
Blackmoorfoot Reservoir
A640
A627
Pennine Way
Mill Stone Edge 443m
Tunnel and Canal Centre
Marsden
Hall Dike
Honley
A616
A6024
B6107
B6108
Meltham
Tunnel
PEAK DISTRICT NATIONAL PARK
Netherthong
West Nab 500m
A6052
Harrop Dale
Delph
A670
SADDLEWORTH MOOR
Wessenden Head
A635
Holmfirth
Anstonley
Cartworth
Dobcross
Saddleworth
Pennine Way
Holmbridge
Uppermill
Brownhill Visitor Centre
Black Hill
Holme
A669
Binn Green
Canal
Dove Stone Reservoir
Drive Route
Picnic Site
Tourist Information
Art Gallery/Museum
0
5 kms
0
Approximate Scale
3 Miles
National Park Boundary
Land above 250 metres (800ft approx)
Land below 250 metres (800ft approx)
Lakes / Reservoirs

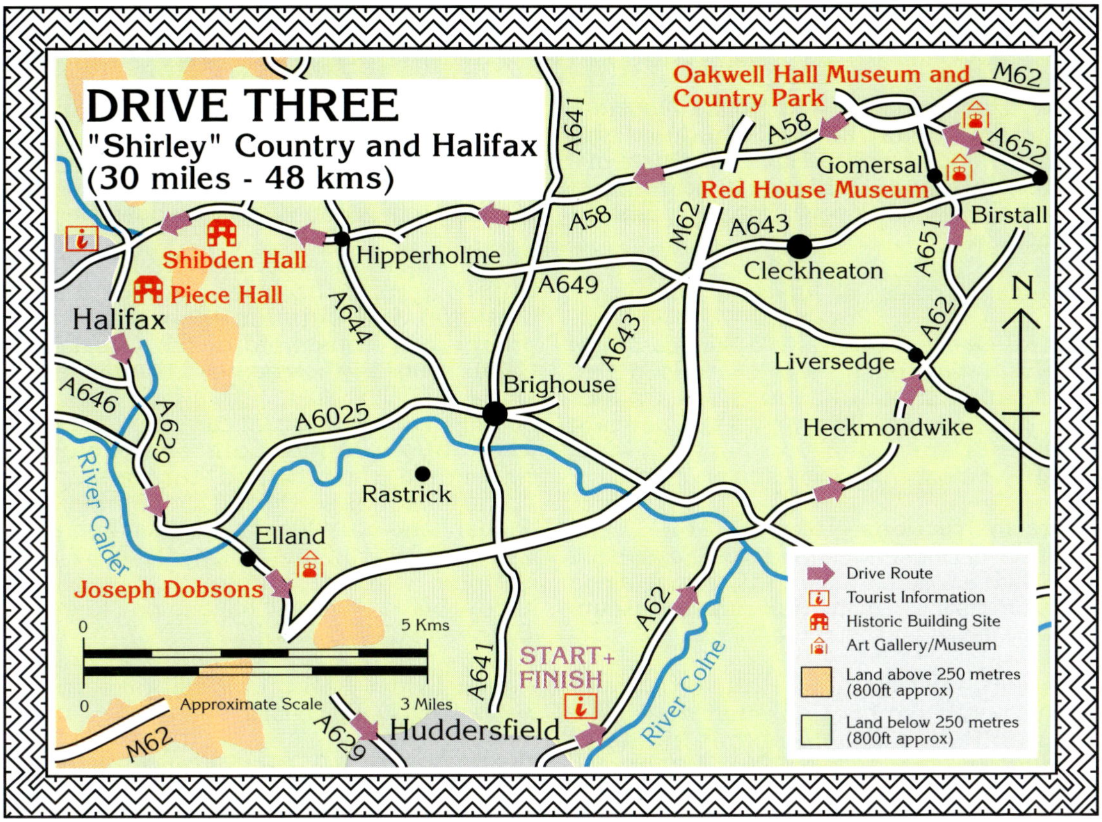
DRIVE THREE
"Shirley" Country and Halifax
(30 miles - 48 kms)
Oakwell Hall Museum and
Country Park
M62
A58
A652
Gomersal
Red House Museum
Birstall
A641
A58
M62
A643
Cleckheaton
A651
Shibden Hall
Piece Hall
Hipperholme
A649
Halifax
A644
A643
A62
Liversedge
N
Brighouse
A646
A629
A6025
Heckmondwike
River Calder
Rastrick
Elland
Joseph Dobsons
0
5 Kms
0
Approximate Scale
3 Miles
M62
A641
START+
FINISH
A629
Huddersfield
A62
River Colne
Drive Route
Tourist Information
Historic Building Site
Art Gallery/Museum
Land above 250 metres
(800ft approx)
Land below 250 metres
(800ft approx)

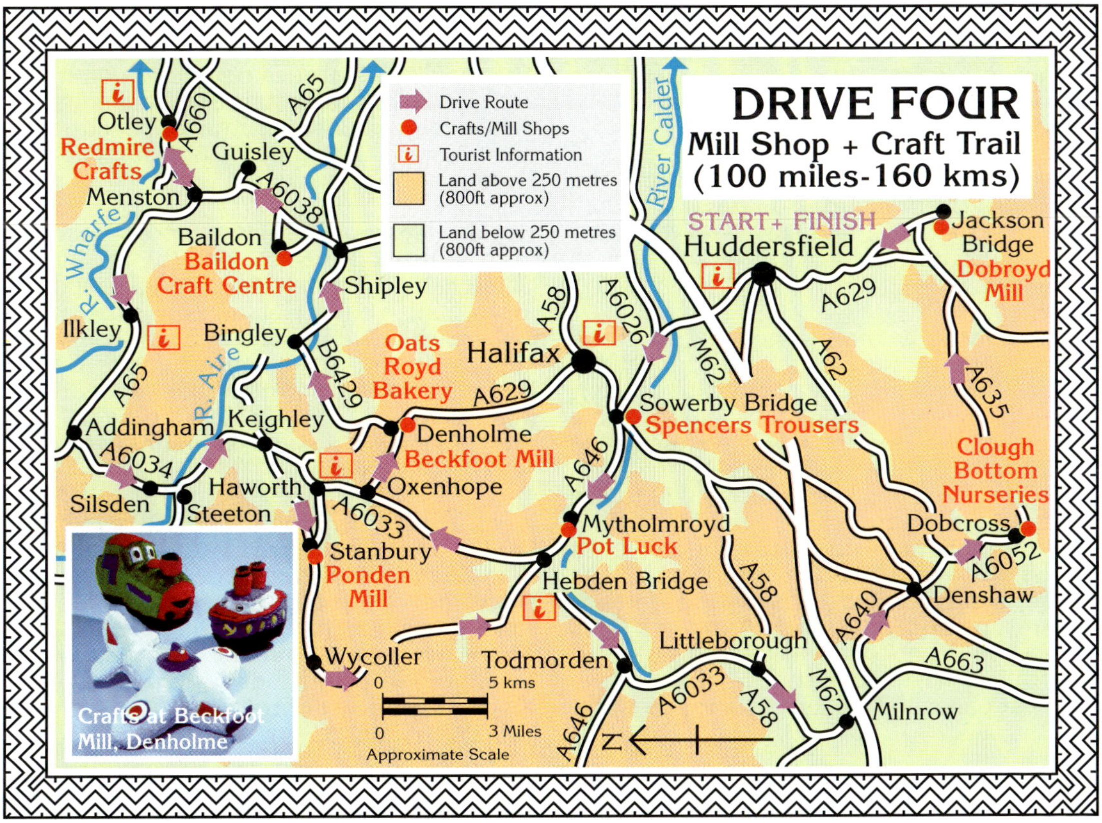
DRIVE FOUR
Mill Shop + Craft Trail
(100 miles-160 kms)
Otley
A660
Redmire
Crafts
Guisley
A65
Menston
A6038
R. Wharfe
Baildon
Baildon
Craft Centre
Shipley
Drive Route
Crafts/Mill Shops
Tourist Information
Land above 250 metres
(800ft approx)
Land below 250 metres
(800ft approx)
River Calder
START+ FINISH
Huddersfield
Jackson
Bridge
Dobroyd
Mill
A629
Ilkley
Bingley
R. Aire
A65
B6429
Oats
Royd
Bakery
Halifax
A58
A6026
A629
M62
A62
A635
Addingham
Keighley
Denholme
Beckfoot Mill
Sowerby Bridge
Spencers Trousers
A6034
Silsden
Steeton
Haworth
Oxenhope
A646
Clough
Bottom
Nurseries
A6033
Mytholmroyd
Pot Luck
Dobcross
Stanbury
Ponden
Mill
Hebden Bridge
A58
A6052
Denshaw
A640
Littleborough
A663
Wycoller
Todmorden
0
5 kms
A6033
A58
M62
Milnrow
0
3 Miles
Approximate Scale
A646
N
Crafts at Beckfoot
Mill, Denholme

Route: Huddersfield - Red House Museum, Gomersal - Oakwell Hall Museum and Country Park - Shibden Hall Folk Museum - Piece Hall and Calderdale Industrial Museum, Halifax - Joseph Dobsons, Elland - Huddersfield

Distance: 30 miles - 48 kms.

General Description: Take a succession of stately homes, each in its own distinctive architectural style, add strong associations with the Brontës, flavour with a delicate tincture of spice and you have 'Shirley' country, a most enjoyable circular drive.

Route Instructions: Take the A62, Leeds road, out of Huddersfield and after about eight miles turn left onto the A651. Continue along it to **Gomersal** where the **Red House Museum** is on the left as you enter the village.

This elegant Georgian Hall, so named because of its red brick construction, is, like Oakwell Hall, a Brontë shrine. Home of Charlotte's great friend, **Mary Taylor**, the house is featured in 'Shirley' as Briarmains and the Taylor family as the 'Yorkes'. Today the rooms are furnished as they would have looked in the 1820s. It is open Monday to Saturday 10am - 5pm, Sunday 1pm - 5pm. Admission is free and you will find it on Oxford Road, Gomersal, Cleckheaton. Telephone (0274) 872165.

Leaving the museum, continue along the A651 towards Bradford. In under a mile turn right onto the A652 and stay on it for half a mile, where you turn left to **Oakwell Hall** as signposted.

This beautifully maintained Elizabethan Manor House is famous for its connections with the Brontës and is featured in Charlotte's novel '**Shirley**' as '**Fieldhead**', home of the heroine, Shirley Keeldar. It is open Monday to Saturday 10am - 5pm, Sunday 1pm - 5pm. Admission, which is free, enables you to see the farm buildings, house exhibitions, and visit the souvenir shop, tea rooms, craft workshops and adventure playground. The house is surrounded by a period garden, arboretum and parkland. And, yes, this Elizabethan manor house is on the telephone: tel. (0924) 474926. Other facilities are a cafe, car parks and toilets, including those for the disabled.

Return towards Bradford on the A652 and the A651. In approximately one mile turn left at a roundabout onto the A58, towards Halifax. Shortly after a junction with the A6036, where there are traffic lights, climb the hill, passing through a road cutting, and take the left hand turn, signposted to **Shibden Hall.**

Superb, half timbered and C15th, Shibden Hall is a must. Its interior gives a very personal and detailed idea of life in a prosperous household of the C17th and C18th. Outside, the courtyard is arranged as an early C19th village with a barn housing a collection of horse-drawn carriages. It is open weekdays 10am - 6pm (5pm closing November - March) and Sundays 2pm - 5pm. It is closed during December and January and open Sundays only in February. Call Shibden Hall the 'West Yorkshire Folk Museum' and the administrators will be happy, but you will still have to pay to get in. Telephone (0422) 52245.

Return to the A58 and it will take you to **Halifax** and its **Piece Hall**.

Until the mid 1970s this gem of C18th architecture was largely unknown outside the area. Now, fully restored to its former glory, this building is perhaps the greatest architectural 'discovery' of our times.

The building's galleries now house craft and antique shops, a restaurant, museum, art gallery and Tourist Information Centre with an open air market in the courtyard on Fridays and Saturdays.

Halifax itself is a largely unspoilt Victorian town with good markets and the fascinating **Calderdale Industrial Museum** adjoining the Piece Hall. Leave Halifax along the A629 towards Huddersfield and at Elland follow the signs into the town centre. Cross Elland Bridge, bear left and take the second right turn, up the hill, past St. Mary's Church. Turn right again for **Joseph Dobsons** who add spice to this drive.

West Yorkshire people refer to sweets as 'spice' and Joseph Dobsons have been manufacturers of traditional boiled sweets since they were established in 1850. The same family has run the business ever since. There are group tours of the factory, by arrangement, and these include tea and biscuits and a sample of their famous Yorkshire mixtures.

Return to the A629 and continue to **Huddersfield.**

Route: Huddersfield - Sowerby Bridge - Mytholmroyd - Denholme - Baildon - Haworth - Hebden Bridge - Saddleworth - Huddersfield

Distance: 100 miles - 160 kms.

General Description: The Mill Shops of the South Pennines reflect its character. This 'Mill Shops and Craft Trail' drive does rather more than that. It links some of the best Mill Shops with one of the most scenic roads in the South Pennines, an irresistible journey that will remain in the memory for years to come.

Route Instructions: Before leaving Huddersfield, visit the **Dobroyd Mill Shop,** Jackson Bridge, for it encapsulates the flavour of the drive ahead. All types of knitwear and knitting yarn are sold there along with leather goods and a good selection of ladies' and gents' clothing.

From Huddersfield take the A629 which goes under the M62, beyond which it splits. Here take the A6026 to Sowerby Bridge, where **Spencers Trousers,** at Friendly Works, Burnley Road is sited. Here the service is indeed friendly and there is a lot on offer.

From Sowerby Bridge take the A58 towards Halifax and on reaching the A646 turn left along it to Mytholmroyd where, at the Old Fire Station Pottery, Cray Road, **Pot Luck** awaits you. Simply trust in Pot Luck and you won't be disappointed. Continue along the A646 to Hebden Bridge where go right, as signposted, along the A6033 to cross Oxenhope Moor into Oxenhope. Turn right at the crossroads along the B6141 to reach the A629 to the south of Denholme and turn left into it for a mouth-watering visit to **Oats Royd Bakery,** Keelham in Denholme.

Here, you can also visit **Beckfoot Mill,** housed in the Clock Mill, which is right in the middle of the place. This is the place for bargains in quilts, cushions and sleeping bags, with genuine manufacturer's seconds on offer at competitive prices.

Leave Denholme along the A629 and in almost a mile go right along the B6429, through **Callingworth,** straight over the cross roads to join the A650 on the western edge of Bingley, from where the way is right, through Shipley, next door, to visit the **Baildon Craft Centre,** Browgate, Baildon. There they can spin a good yarn and usually manage to come up with something you've always wanted but never had the chance to purchase until now. Leave Baildon northwards, along the A6038 into Guiseley, where you go left along the A65 to Menston, where you go right, briefly, into **Otley,** there to find at No 10 Kirkgate Arcade, **Redmire Crafts.**

Take the A659 westwards, out of Otley to join and continue along the A65 through pleasant Ilkley to Addingham, village where you turn left along the A6034 to join the A629 at Glusburn and go left, along it, through Keighley, and south, following roughly the line of the Keighley and Worth Valley Railway on the right. When the A629 turns sharp left at Cross Roads, go sharp right, edging **Haworth,** turn right again to go under the Worth Valley line and take the first turning on the right to **Ponden Mill,** Stanbury, near Lower Laithes Reservoir where a welcome awaits you. Here you can purchase continental quilts, household furnishings, clothing and toys. And if selecting from this lot brings on an appetite, they have a restaurant.

Leave by continuing westward along a scenic, minor road that cuts between Keighley Moor to the north and Widdop Moor to the south, running for most of the way parallel to the **Brontë Way** on your left. Soon after passing Water Sheddies Reservoir, where the road splits, go left, through Wycoller and at a T-junction turn left along another minor road. Take the next turning on your left, as you edge the **Forest of Trawden,** following a scenic route. The road, now running roughly westwards, meanders, then makes a sharp right turn and continues in a south westerly direction to a T-junction at Coldwell Reservoirs. Go left, re-crossing Widdup Moor, much further south, to reach **Hebden Bridge**. Here, as signposted, go right, along the A646 to **Todmorden,** where go left, along the A6033 to **Littleborough.** Turn right here, along the A58 and follow the first left, the A664, to a crossroads, where turn left, through **Milnrow,** and under the M62, just beyond which go left along the A640, to **Denshaw** and continue southwards to signposted **Saddleworth** where, having sampled some of the most scenic roads in the South Pennines, **Clough Bottom Nurseries and Garden Centre** merits a visit. The Garden Centre is in a woodland setting and there are farm animals, a farm implements museum, a picnic area and tea gardens. Continue along the A62, back to **Huddersfield,** the end of a super, scenic drive.

SPENCERS TROUSERS

The history of the South Pennines is closely bound up with craftwork - the home-based textile crafts of spinning and weaving were at the root of the region's prosperity.

It comes as no surprise, therefore, to find a strong interest in crafts and craftwork still, particularly as, here no less than elsewhere in the country, the 'green movement' has brought in its wake a revived interest in hand-operated, non-polluting techniques and 'natural' materials. So hand-thrown pottery - as demonstrated at Pot Luck in Hebden Bridge, for instance - home-spun fabrics, hand-made objects crafted from wood and stone are all enjoying a new, wider popularity.

Craft shops and displays can be found in most towns, with the **Piece Hall in Halifax** and the **Towneley Hall Craft Museum in Burnley** being well worth seeking out.

If you are not already a dedicated craft enthusiast - and have not therefore decided what you are looking for - you will welcome the opportunity to explore a good, general selection of crafts, such as will be found at the **Baildon Craft Centre** at Baildon, near Shipley. Here you will find a wide choice of craft products, all carefully selected and attractively displayed.

It is always a pleasure to come away from an area you have been visiting with gifts for others, or indeed a treasure for yourself, made by a local craftsperson. The Baildon Craft Centre may be a good starting point for finding such items and may even introduce you to a whole new area of craftwork which comes to fascinate you and which sets you off in quest of other work by a particular artist or in a particular idiom.

Many of the crafts have very ancient origins indeed, going back to the days when self-sufficient small communities had to make by hand what they needed, and among the oldest and most necessary skills were those of the potter. In this area, not so far from the famous Potteries, these skills are still flourishing today.

A wonderful variety of crafts are on display at **Pot Luck**, which occupies the Old Fire Station at Mytholmroyd, near Hebden Bridge.

Chief among them are the items made by local potter, John Pencheon, who works on the premises producing a wide range of kitchen ware in his own distinctive style. His bowls and mugs are especially popular and indeed, when John is hand-throwing pots on the potter's wheel, a glass partition in the shop allows visitors to view him at work.

Storage pots for everything from bread to garlic and from tea to muesli are available too, as well as a range of terracotta garden pots. Other locally produced items include delicious honey and finely executed pencil drawings of local beauty spots.

Meanwhile Pot Luck lives up to its name, in offering a huge choice of other crafts, including jewellery, wooden toys, badges and games, walking sticks, collectors' plates, mugs and wall plaques, fine porcelain and china ornaments, mirrors, mobiles and even woollen rugs and items of clothing such as shawls and scarves, capes and jackets.

All crafts are of British origin, many produced by craftspeople working in the local area, and the originality of the selection often draws favourable comment from visitors.

Equally essential were the skills of the woodworker, who fashioned everything from large pieces of furniture to much smaller items such as bowls, tool handes and so on. The pleasure to be gained from a well made wooden article has today come to be valued anew, after decades of machine produced items, and wooden toys in particular are enjoying renewed popularity.

Visitors looking for something different will find in **Woodworks** a traditional toyshop that actually makes toys as well as selling them.

All the old favourites are stocked - rocking horses, forts, castles, garages, farms, hobby-horses, puzzles, pull-alongs, push-alongs, whip and top, and many more - all in wood and made locally.

There is also a wide range of dolls' houses - for under-fives to over-sixty-fives! - together with a large selection of miniatures to suit all pockets. Furniture is made to one sixteenth and one twelfth scale, and attracts a large number of collectors.

Children's furniture and a wide choice of gifts for all ages complete the catalogue.

Specialist producer of Commemorative China mugs, plates, plaques etc, for Churches, Schools, Fundraising and the retail giftware trade. Any quantity happily quoted for

&

Wholesaler of stoneware kitchen and decorative items all hand-thrown on the premises.

OPENING HOURS
Monday - Saturday (incl): 9a.m. - 5p.m.
Telephone STELLA UNDERHILL on
HALIFAX (0422) 883651

WOODWORKS

KIRKGATE ARCADE
OTLEY

Doll's Houses

Miniatures

• • •

Things in Wood

Large Range of Toys & Gifts

(0943) 850261 - (0274) 594946

Also Most Sundays
at Baildon Craft Centre

Baildon Craft Centre

Browgate, Baildon, Shipley,
West Yorkshire, BD17 6BP
Tel: 0274 594946

We take great pleasure in inviting you to visit the most unique working craft centre in the north. We are housed in an old but imposing former Primitive Methodist Chapel on the edge of the famous Rombalds Moor (commonly known as Ilkley Moor) in the village of Baildon. You will find that many of the items on display and for sale have been made on the premises and you can often see them being made.

Available in the centre:
Silk Painting • Stained Glass • Printing • • Candles • Pyrography • Pottery • Craft Kits • Wooden Toys• Christening Gowns • Leather Goods • Yorkshire Stone Cottages • Decoupage Kits • Upholstery • Dressmaking and Alterations • Silk and Dried Flowers • Patchwork Cushions and Bedding • Soft Toys • Sweaters • Kites.

We also have a Coffee Shop and Toilet Facilities.
Open Tuesday - Sunday 10am - 5pm.

OATS ROYD BAKERY

KEELHAM, DENHOLME, BRADFORD
WEST YORKSHIRE BD13 4HH
Telephone Bradford 833149
ASA NICHOLSON & SONS

Asa Nicholsons's Tearoom at the bakery gives you an opportunity to watch the bakers whilst you eat. Designed with the idea that you can see the food being prepared. Quality and hygiene being our main concern we hope to give satisfaction. This is a non-smoking tearoom.

The airconditioned tearoom has seating for 50, plus 2 high-chairs. Filtered Yorkshire water hopefully gives you a good cup of tea or coffee. We have an extensive menu with all our own made cakes, savouries, pizzas, bread etc. Complimented with chips, salad and all-day breakfast.

At the planning stage of the tearoom we considered the disabled. There is easy access with special disabled toilets and good parking. With the family firm having been in business for over 90 years, we had to have a nostalgic theme in the decorations and photographs. These we hope will add interest to your visit.

Some toys are educational by design, but all develop and encourage constructive play and imagination, in addition to looking good and being fun to play with. Toys from Woodworks are the kind that become family heirlooms, they retain their attractions, and they last.

Woodworks' 'plastic-free' experience can be enjoyed in an attractive Edwardian Arcade of shops in Otley, an historic market town known as the Gateway to Wharfedale, and the town itself is well worth a visit.

By no means least among the local skills that were so necessary was that of the gardener or cultivator of plants and vegetables. Gardening, too, 'back to the soil in miniature', is experiencing a boom time - witness the spread of the garden centre concept - with the challenge of growing plants in different environments being eagerly met by the gardeners who throng to establishments like **Clough Bottom Nurseries**.

Here you will not only find all you need for your garden but you can enjoy a break in the coffee shop, where all the cakes are home made - a true taste of the South Pennines! And, of course, returning home with a few plants ensures that you will have a living souvenir of your visit to this region which will give you pleasure for years to come.

The region has many excellent gardens to explore, both those which are open on a regular basis and many more which open on a few days a year in aid of the **National Gardens Scheme**. The former are listed in the Directory section at the end of this guide. For information about the latter, please enquire at TICs, who will have a list of opening dates in their area, or look for a copy of the famous 'yellow book', published annually by the National Gardens Scheme and sold through most bookshops.

Having recently mentioned home-baked fare, let us now turn to a place where the main focus is on just that.

Oats Royd Bakery, Keelham

The Tea Room and Bakery Shop of Asa Nicholson and Sons' **Oats Royd Bakery** at Keelham offer ample evidence that a person being forced to change the way he makes his living is not a new situation, and can turn out very well indeed!

Towards the end of the last century, the young Asa Nicholson was employed clearing sites in preparation for stone quarrying. The winter of 1898 was so harsh that the ground was frozen solid for many weeks, and quarrying work was halted, putting Asa out of work.

Whilst he was searching for other employment, his sister, Eva, suggested that he tried his hand at baking **Oat Bread** (an oval pancake-like bread in slices made from oats). She was sure that they would sell easily.

Asa asked around the neighbourhood to find someone to teach him the trade; eventually T.H. Binns Esq. of Halifax agreed to help him. The training cost £5.00 plus 1 farthing fine for every oatcake that was spoilt. Fortunately Asa learned quickly and was soon able to sell all the oat bread he made, by calling door to door on his way home each evening.

A 'Bakestun' or Bakestone (hot plate) was soon acquired and Asa set up his own small bakery at **Bottomley Holes** (Bod'oiles to the locals), about quarter of a mile from the present site. As the business prospered, a horse and cart was bought for deliveries.

By the 1920s, Asa's sons, Clifford and Wilfrid, had joined the expanding business and started making bread and other items. As a result, Asa Nicholson and Sons was one of the first businesses in the area to buy a motor vehicle for deliveries (a second-hand Model T Ford converted from a car to a flat waggon).

The old bakery at 'Bod'oiles' had always been a ramshackle affair in converted cottages and plans were made for a new bakery. In 1947 the business moved to the present site, named Oats Royd Bakery, in the centre of **Keelham.**

Since that date the bakery has been modernised and extended and currently produces a hundred lines. The business has always been operated as a friendly family affair; it is currently run by Asa's grandson and great-grandson - and continues its success to this day.

Dobroyd Mill Shop, near Hepworth

Mill Shops are becoming an increasing attraction, both because of the wide range of goods and bargains they offer, and the interesting buildings in which they are housed. Here we have room to feature only a few of the very many mills in the region.

Dobroyd Mills was built at the turn of the century and this impressive building dominates the small village of Jackson Bridge near Hepworth. Its history accurately reflects the varied fortunes of the British Textile Industry during the past 100 years.

The original Dobroyd Mills Co. Ltd. operated as a 'vertical' mill where raw materials such as cotton and wool were transformed from their raw state into finished garments within the one site. As with most late Victorian and early Edwardian Mills, their power sources were water and labour. Indeed during their peak the Mills employed well over 300 people, and the little cottages within Jackson Bridge housed many of these workers - not surprisingly the Mill owner's house was built overlooking his minions and this Gothic example is situated on the hill between Jackson Bridge and New Mill.

With the **technological advances** made during the Second World War, the way of life on which Dobroyd Mills had depended altered considerably. Indeed labour was more mobile, better educated and had greater aspirations. Allied to these changes at home was the generation of Third World Countries producing vast quantities of textiles at very low cost. The days for Dobroyd Mills Co. Ltd. were numbered and a slow decline ensued.

During the 1970s, John Woodhead Ltd. purchased the Mills and began production of fine quality yarns of which they are justly proud, including Cashmere, Lambswool and Angora blends. Such is their reputation that they supply the top quality knitters of England and Scotland.

In 1983, John Woodhead opened their **Dobroyd Mill Shop** which stocks many knitwear items made from their own yarns. The shop also stocks a fine selection of blazers, trousers, shirts, blouses, skirts and hosiery - many produced in Yorkshire. The shop has proved to be a popular stop for tourists, not only for the bargains to be had, but also its close proximity to the Last of the Summer Wine Pub, 'The White Horse'. Indeed The Dobroyd Mills and the village of Jackson Bridge proves to be one of those fascinating backwaters which constantly surprise the visitor on his or her tour through the North of England.

Beckfoot Mill, Denholme

Beckfoot Mill are well-known handicraft suppliers who specialise in polyester fillings and waddings. Established in the 1930s, the business has always been involved in handling and processing fibres, both natural and man-made.

No longer situated at the original mill on Harden beck, they are now to be found on their parent company's site in the centre of Denholme. **Pennine Fibre Industries** are the only UK company to manufacture polyester fibre and much of this comes from re-cycled industrial polymer waste, backing up the environmental-friendly involvement to conserve the earth's resources.

Clock Mill, a magnificent Victorian building (complete with clock tower), can easily be seen as it stands on the main Halifax to Keighley road (A629), and the mill shop entrance is directly under the clock. There is a car-park for visitors nearby.

A wide range of soft-toy patterns and kits have been developed in connection with the filling fibre and these are to be found displayed in the mill shop along with many other materials and accessories used in toy-making, such as fur fabrics, felt, eyes, noses and joints.

Other **handicraft materials** such as plastic canvas, patchwork templates and wadding, sewing requisites, tapestry and embroidery kits are augmented with instruction booklets, enabling those in search of a satisfying hobby to 'have a go'. Children's handicraft kits and games are also available.

There are very good bargains to be had in quilts, both perfects and 'seconds' from a sister manufacturer, also pillows and sleeping bags. A range of other textile based goods are kept and coach parties are welcomed by arrangement. Help and advice is readily given by experienced staff.

Every year thousands of people from all over the world make the journey to the charming Yorkshire village of Haworth, home of the famous Brontë Parsonage and close to the Keighley and Worth Valley Railway.

In the last decade, however, another carefully restored part of Yorkshire's great industrial heritage is proving to be just as popular with visitors as Haworth.

Just a short distance out of the village, stands **Ponden Mill**, once one of the largest working mills in the country in the days when Yorkshire's textile industry was at its peak, and the yarns and cloths produced here were famous all over the world.

Sadly many of the mills from that great age no longer exist. Decline in the textile industry has meant that many have had to close, their buildings neglected and allowed to fall into disrepair. Others have been demolished to make way for modern development, with a large irreplaceable part of the social and industrial history of the area being lost for evermore in the process.

Thankfully that was not the case with Ponden Mill. Over ten years ago this great local landmark was given a new lease of life when, after careful and faithful restoration, it was turned into a **unique retailing centre**. Today the Mill is the flagship of a growing network of Ponden Mill high street shops, stretching out across the country.

In the last eighteen months the original Ponden Mill near Haworth has once again been completely refurbished and renovated, to provide over fifty percent more space to facilitate the display of an even wider range of merchandise, making the Ponden Mill Centre arguably the largest retailer of quality **home linens and furnishing** anywhere in the North of England. Visitors to the new, spacious Ponden Mill will find it even more of a treasure trove for bargains and superb merchandise than it was before.

In addition to their extensive 'own label' range of linens, Ponden Mill continues to offer tremendous savings on all the top name brands such as Dorma, Sheridan and Chortex. For shoppers looking to achieve a totally colour co-ordinated look in their homes, be it bedroom or bathroom, Ponden offers a very comprehensive selection of the very best in matching linens, fabrics and towellings.

Thanks to their massive bulk buying powers, Ponden is in a position to market many of these items to its customers at exceptionally low prices. In addition Ponden Mill is able to source a wide selection of 'seconds' and manufacturers' 'end of ranges' and these are regularly available at bargain prices for the discerning shopper.

However, the now greatly expanded Ponden Mill Centre is much more than just a source of the finest and best textiles one can buy.

The Centre is packed with a host of **furnishing ideas and stylish products**, bound to attract and delight all those who are looking for inspiration in how to improve the interior decoration and the design of their homes.

Visitors browsing round will discover a wealth of table linens, lace work, table decorations and attractive decorative ware, all designed to enhance the home and give it that extra bit of flair.

Ponden's extensive display of **cane and wickerwork** products now has even more floor space, and includes many designs not previously on display, which are ideal for adding that individual finishing touch to a room.

The **Country Clothing** section at the Ponden Mill Centre has also been enlarged and now contains an even more varied selection of top quality, chunky knit woollens and hard wearing tweeds and sheepskins, ideal for keeping one snug and warm in even the coldest winter weather.

And when they are tired of browsing, visitors can always drop into the **Weavers' Restaurant** and enjoy a well earned cup of tea and some of the tasty home cooked cakes and scones available there, or tuck into one of the delicious stand pies, a local delicacy for which the restaurant is justifiably famous.

However, before leaving, visitors will find it well worthwhile to pay one last visit to the Centre's well stocked **craft gift shop**.

It's here, among the many hundreds of items on display, that they will surely find that special something that will make the perfect present for a friend or relative, or a treasured memento of their own memorable day out at the Ponden Mill Centre.

Hebden Lodge Hotel

"A modest exterior hides a wealth of true professional hotel management. The comfort, care and well being of their guests is paramount. The food and its presentation is of the highest quality. Hebden Bridge should be proud of the standard set by this small hotel."

Mr and Mrs Mitchell 3rd September 1990
(Extract from the Hebden Lodge Hotel visitors book.)

Christine and Robert, Chef Patron of this attractive Hotel, offer you comfortable accommodation in the heart of the Calder and Hebden Valley's, a perfect base for exploring the South Pennines.

We offer everything you are looking for whilst away from home, be it on business, holiday or that much needed weekend break.
All the rooms are en-suite and include colour television, direct dial telephone (which includes baby listening) radio alarms, hot drinks facilities, and hairdryers. There are downstairs bedrooms suitable for the disabled with easy access to all public rooms. All rooms are individually furnished and decorated to a high standard.

Our five course table d'hote dinner menu offers an extensive choice covering English, French, and Italian cuisines, cooked for you by Robert, Chef Patron. With the menu changed daily, we promise you will not be disappointed. Special diets can be catered for including vegetarian.

Our dedicated staff are friendly and efficient and work hard at making your stay a happy and comfortable one.

For Brochure telephone: 0422 - 845272 or write to : Hebden Lodge Hotel, New Road, Hebden Bridge, West Yorkshire, HX7 8AD.

English Tourist Board · Les Routiers · AA ★★

Cross Stone Road, Todmorden

The Berghof Hotel, as its name implies (House on a Mountain) stands in the elevated village of Cross Stone enjoying splendid panoramic views of the surrounding Pennine Hills with the town of Todmorden below. Formally the Bay Horse Inn circa 1714 steeped in local history, one of the oldest licensed premises in the Calderale area, now thoughtfully converted to bring to you a taste of Austrian hospitality and Gemutlichkeit.
The Austrian Chef/proprietor Peter Brandstatter and his wife Kathy have created in the Berghof restaurant a scene straight from an Austrian Gasthof, from the waitresses in their colourful dirndls to the brightly painted pelmets, wood floors and pine furnishings. Serving traditional Austrian specialities together with International cuisine, the restaurant has gained a reputation of excellence and friendliness which combine to make it the perfect venue for that special occasion.
In addition to the Berghof Restaurant the Jager Stube (Hunters Lodge) offers alternative cuisine. Classic Game Dishes, Austrian and English Cuisine. A popular gathering place for that informal business lunch or for that evening out with friends. The Jager Stube also provides the perfect setting for Wedding Receptions and Parties, catering for up to 70 guests.
6 Ensuite bedrooms and an exquisite Bridal Suite. All furnished with Original Austrian Antiques yet offering 20th Century Comforts.
A la Carte and Table d'hote menus available. Large Car Park. Open for Lunch & Dinner.
Reservations advisable. Telephone (0706) 812966.

You will travel through time in **Calderdale,** discovering the whole **history of the great British Woollen Industry** in this spectacular area. Old weaving settlements can still be found along the 'causey stones', ancient packhorse routes across the Pennine moors, along which weavers carried their 'pieces' of cloth to the magnificent **Piece Hall in Halifax** - a unique building reminiscent of some of the grandest Italian piazzas, once the centre of all textile trading activity and now a mixture of shops, galleries, museums and markets. You can step into the tranquillity of **Shibden Hall** and see life as far back as the C15th including the 'Crispin Inn' where Luddite riots were planned; enjoy the boats and trains in the surrounding park or see fine textile and military displays in Halifax's **Bankfield Museum**.

The **Rochdale Canal,** opened in 1804 and navigable until 50 years ago, has now been carefully restored, and you can enjoy horse-drawn cruises and holiday boat hire passing through spectacular Pennine scenery. Horse power was also essential in towns and **Horses at Work** in Halifax, with its rides and other attractions, shows just this. In Halifax, the 'town of a hundred trades', the **Calderdale Industrial Museum,** next to the Piece Hall, this museum clatters, hisses and glides as its working exhibits depict work and life in this great Pennine town, said to have the finest Victorian town centre in the North of England. Other towns worth exploring include **Brighouse, Elland, Sowerby Bridge, Hebden Bridge** and **Todmorden.**

Near **Hebden Bridge** is the only place in Britain still making clogs, **Walkley's Clog Mill.** In the town itself are **Childhood Reflections** and the **Hebden Crypt,** as well as a good selection of art and craft shops, while, just up at Old Town outside Hebden Bridge is **Automobilia Motor Museum.**

Walking opportunities in Calderdale are endless and with the books and walks on offer in the TICs in Todmorden, Hebden Bridge and Halifax you really are spoilt for choice. Visit the **North Dean Nature Centre** at West Vale, the start of the 50 mile (80 km) Calderdale Way, to see more about Calderdale's countryside or enjoy the vast expanse of **Ogden Water**, north of Halifax. Alternatively, how about tacking up and exploring **Calderdale on horseback**, pedalling around the 150 mile (240 km) **West Yorkshire Cycle Route**, or paddling your canoe down **Sowerby Bridge's slalom course?** Calderdale - once discovered, never forgotten -you'll soon see why.

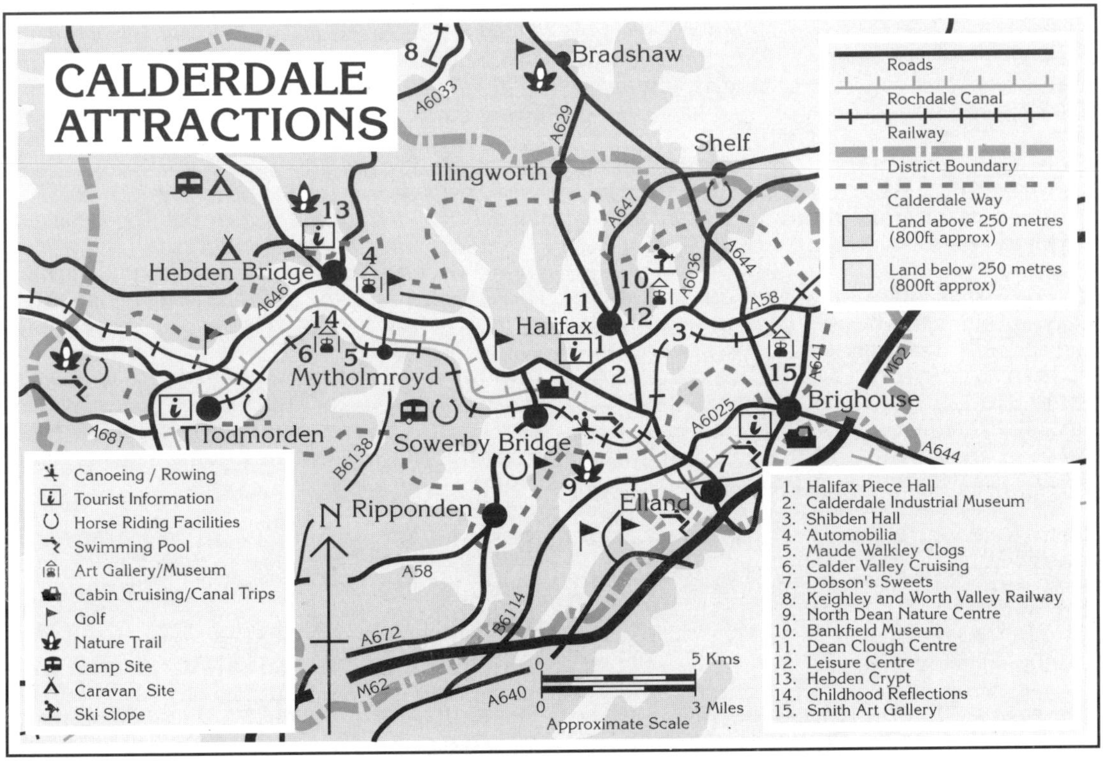

Haworth looks onto a moorland that for most of the year lies **brooding and desolate,** its vast wastes scarred with black quarries and littered with broken rocks and coarse grasses. Only when the heather is in bloom does the melancholy fade..... only then is the unspeakable loneliness assuaged.

Haworth, although as tristful as its surroundings, is one of the **best loved and most visited villages** in the South Pennines. Today its mills and houses and the steep, narrow street up which, long ago, came Patrick Brontë with his Cornish wife, their six children and seven cartloads of furniture, hold a very special place in English literature.

The Brontë family was touched with brilliance, with Emily the most brilliant of all. Her 'Wuthering Heights', though not recognised as such to begin with, was destined to become one of the **most powerful and dramatic novels** ever written in the English language. It was this tour-de-force, along with the immortal works of her sisters Charlotte and Anne, that turned obscure Haworth into literary lodestone.

It was during the spring of 1820 that the Brontës came to Haworth. Frail Maria, Patrick's wife, who **loathed the place** and pined for her Cornish home, died at Haworth the following year, as did little Maria and her sister, Elizabeth, who were still children.

From a very early age, the three remaining sisters enjoyed writing and with their brother, Branwell, produced a **mass of budding epics** which they called 'Gondal'.

In 1846, the sisters published a book of poems under the names of Currer, Ellis and Acton Bell - but only **two copies were sold!** Within the next two years, in 1847, Charlotte had an immediate success with what was to become her masterpiece, 'Jane Eyre'. Later that same year Emily's 'Wuthering Heights' was published.

Then followed a series of **disasters**. Both Branwell, who had become addicted to drink and drugs, and Emily died in 1848. Then in 1849, Anne, who had published two novels, 'Agnes Grey' and 'The Tenant of Wildfell Hall', also died.

Charlotte's second novel, 'Shirley', was published in 1849 and in 1853 'Villette' appeared, but, in 1855, after **less than a year** of married life, she died in childbirth.

Behind their parsonage home a rough track leads onto the moor. The three sisters would tread along this path to escape their unsympathetic Aunt Elizabeth. One of the glens they frequented contains a waterfall which now bears the Brontë name. At this **secluded spot** there stands a large stone known as the Brontë's Chair, where they would rest and tell tales to one another. Higher on the moor is ruinous Top Withens, the site for 'Wuthering Heights'.

Haworth stands between these moors and the busy Worth Valley. The Church, the Inn and the Parsonage huddle around the churchyard at the top of the street. Of the church, only the tower remains from Brontë days. The stony little hill to the Brontë home is no longer **'a little and a lone green lane that opened on a common wide'**, as Emily put it; instead a rather splendid sign, prominently displayed, draws people to the Brontë home.

The view from the Parsonage is depressing: iron railings enclosing a few shading trees and a confusion of black gravestones. Sir James Roberts, a native of Haworth, **purchased the Parsonage** for the Brontë Society and a new wing has been added and some changes made to its interiors. There are highly contentious plans for a new museum building, but the rooms on view are much as the sisters knew them. Upstairs is the tiny nursery in which they spent the few happy hours they knew. This is the most appealing room in the house. It contains the cradle in which the little sisters were rocked to sleep. **Faint pencil scrawls** and pictures they painted can be seen on the walls. It was a special place and Charlotte wrote of it, 'pen cannot portray the deep interest of scenes I have witnessed in that little room with the long, narrow bed and the bare whitewashed walls'. Throughout the house the rooms are full of intimate, small things.

Sad memories fill this grim Parsonage, whose very walls reek of suffering and struggle. But for all that, it is **a house of pilgrimage** for all who cherish these indomitable sisters, whose spirits would not be quenched by adversity and whose combined genius burned with such a fierce flame that it brought English literature to new heights.

'Odersfelt' - that is how the name is given in the ancient Norman Domesday Book - and even traces of earlier Roman life can be found. Yet Huddersfield is also a modern, **typically Yorkshire town**, full of unsuspected qualities, strong traditions and attractive buildings; set in the middle of outstanding countryside.

Its reputation was built around the textile industry and today it is the main centre for fancy woollen goods, for no place makes finer cloth than Huddersfield. It is **world famous** for its worsted and woollen fabrics and its silk and cotton goods. Engineering, the manufacture of chemicals and dye stuffs, machinery and tools are also carried out, with firms like Guy Christian and Ramsden Landing giving diversity.

Huddersfield, still a 'little town' when Richard Pococke called there in the C18th, really began to **develop** during the C18th and C19th. In 1766 its great Cloth Hall was built, largely due to the efforts of the Lords of the Manor, the Ramsden family, who developed the town and gained Royal Assent to hold a market there. The family also built the Ramsden Canal and the railway.

The railway station, completed in 1850, heralded the **development of a new town** with substantial elegant buildings built of local quarried sandstone from Crosland Moor.

Work began on the building of **the Town Hall** in 1878 just preceding confirmation of County Borough status in 1888. Its structure is in Italian style, relieved with pilasters and columns supporting a cornice and pediments. The public library and art gallery, in contrast, is a huge building designed by E.H. Ashburner, with figures representing the inspiration of Literature and Art, sculpted by James Woodford, and two panels of sculpture in relief, symbolic of Navigation, Engineering, Song and Dance, History, Bird Life, Tragedy, Music and Poetry.

The front of **the railway station,** adorned with eight fluted columns, faces St. George's Square, the focal point of the 'new town'. Apart from the railway facade, considered by many people to be the finest in England, the square is bounded by the George Hotel, the Yorkshire Building Society and Lion Chambers. Many of the warehouses and offices in the square were built by the eminent British architect Sir William Tike in the **Italianate style,** which magnificently conceals their industrial use.

The Church of **St. Peter is** not far away, in the very heart of the town. It is an imposing C15th style building, built in the C19th and it stands where the Lacy family are supposed to have founded a church in Norman times.

In 1920 probably the most significant event, in Huddersfield's history took place when its Corporation purchased **the Ramsden Estate,** including almost all the town centre from Sir J.F. Ramsden, the sixth Baronet. As a result of this, Huddersfield has affectionately been styled as the 'the town that bought itself'.

One of the town's **open spaces**, Greenhead Park, houses an impressive **War Memorial.** Another, Beaumont Park, sited high above the town and the thirty arched viaduct over the River Holme, contains charming **woodlands** and rocks. Golmscar Woods, in springtime, are carpeted with bluebells. In Norman Park, in a hollow beside a stream there is a monument of a soldier, placed there in memory of all who died for peace. Crowning Almondsbury Hill, the most striking natural landmark in the area and which has been occupied since the Stone Age, is the **Jubilee Tower**. Built in the year 1898-99 to celebrate the 60th anniversary of Queen Victoria's reign, the top of its tower stands almost 300 metres (1,000 ft) above sea level. From it there are splendid panoramic views. Inside, an exhibition traces the hill's 4,000 years of history.

Recently the town has been **improved** by the construction of the Inner Ring Road, the creation of new pedestrianised shopping streets, the expansion of the Technical College and the creation of the Polytechnic. When in 1974, local government was reorganised, Huddersfield was chosen as the **administrative headquarters** of Kirklees Metropolitan Economic Development Unit from Kirklees House in Market Street.

In 1981 the population of Huddersfield was 123,168 and, with easy access to the countryside of the South Pennines, good housing, shopping and entertainment, the town is increasingly becoming a popular place for visitors and an ideal place in which to live and work.

Rochdale, which takes its name from the Roch, the river it straddles, sits comfortably on the edge of the impressive Rossendale Fells. Its strength lies more in its proud spirit, as expressed in its **fine public buildings,** than in its natural charms.

Last century Rochdale gave England one of the noblest figures ever to sit in its Parliament and one of the most powerful ideas ever to shape democratic government.

The man was **John Bright** (1811-1889), the son of a Quaker Rochdale mill owner, who became Cobden's Chief Lieutenant in the Anti-Corn-Law League, which he joined in 1830. In 1834 he entered Parliament where his oratory soon made him notable, and he held office in Gladstone's cabinets of 1868 and 1880.

The idea was **the Co-operative Movement**. In 1844 twenty artisans opened a store in Toad Lane to supply themselves with provisions. Their joint capital was £28.00 subscribed by weekly sums of twopence or threepence. Flour, oatmeal, butter, sugar, and candles were at first the only items dealt with in the store. Co-operative groups had been formed before, but the Rochdale pioneers, mostly cotton weavers, set the pattern which has been closely followed by a thousand Co-ops, here and abroad, up to the present day.

Their main features were **distribution of profits** among members according to the value of their purchases of goods, the payment of a fixed rate of interest on capital, no share in profits coming to the subscribers of capital as such, and democratic control, each member having one vote whatever his capital holding.

From a huddle of squalid old buildings and a foul river, the local authorities, pioneering a great public scheme setting to work its unemployed, created a fine new town centre. Now, there is a splendid new road, the Esplanade, public gardens, a spacious square and an imposing group of buildings.

The **town hall** is superb; it covers over 2,500 square metres (3,000 sq yds) and is 84 metres (92 yds) long. Its tower, 58 metres (190 ft) high and with a clock in its square lantern, has been compared with Big Ben tower at Westminster. Inside there is a vaulted room called the Exchange and a fine, carved staircase, which leads to a medieval style chamber with a magnificent panelled roof carried by sixteen angels. A huge fresco, measuring 10½ by 4½ metres (35 by 15 ft), depicts King John signing the Magna Carta, watched by Stephen Longton and the barons. The Great Hall contains more than 30 life size portraits of our kings and queens since the Norman Conquest.

From St Chad's Church, reached by 122 steps, or the nearby stocks, there is a **fine view** of the town and the surrounding hills. Buried beneath one of the flat tombstones in the churchyard is John Collier, the earliest of all Lancashire's dialect poets. Using the pen name 'Tom Bobbin', he was also a weaver, schoolmaster and painter - the 'Lancashire Hogarth'.

The slender arches inside the Church are C13th and the font is C15th. Perhaps the most striking aspect of St Chad's is the variety of high quality woodwork, from roofs to furniture of different periods. Much of the church was renewed during the C19th.

There is a morbid C17th copper plate in an aisle which shows two **grisly skeletons** mouthing the words:

> 'As you are, so were we: As we are, so must you be'.

Sir James Kay-Shuttleworth, founder of our **English system of education** was a son of Rochdale, as were **Samuel Turner**, famed for his research into the manufacturing properties of asbestos, **Professor John Mills,** the great authority on earthquakes, and **Sir Henry Howarth**, geologist and antiquary. **Sir Cyril Smith**, heavyweight MP for Rochdale, was also born there.

Born there in 1898, Grace Stansfield is perhaps Rochdale's most famous daughter. As **Gracie Fields,** singer and comedienne, she used her inimitable voice and personality, Lancashire humour and high spirits to lift the spirits of the working class audiences through the depression years of the thirties.

Today's Rochdale offers a warm Lancashire welcome to all its visitors and invites them to emulate 'Our Gracie's' inducement to 'Sing as we go'; for these days there is a lot to sing about in Rochdale.

Bradford was once **a little sheep-raising town** set in a hollow of the hills, marketing home grown fleeces and making cloth on handlooms. Then came steam and with it the power loom and Bradford's prosperity. Now its trade is world wide.

It is the world's **central market for wool** and woollen products. Five sixths of England's wool business is carried out at Bradford and it also has a large trade in other fabrics, cotton and silk having become an important part of its industry. The Manningham Mills, where silk and velvet are made, are the biggest of their kind in the world. Many other industries have been developed there, including dyeing and finishing, engineering, machine tools and quarrying.

Bradford has been a **pioneer city** not only in business but also in such social work as hospitals and clinics, school doctors and cheap meals at poor schools. The foundation of our free education system was established by Bradford MP, William Edward Forster.

The **middle of Bradford** has been **reconstructed and modernised,** resulting in the demolition of many old landmarks like the Old Swan Arcade where J.B. Priestley worked as a young man. Morley Street, a fine road running south west from Town Hall Square, slices through some of the oldest parts of the city. The roof of Exchange Station has two 30 metre (100 ft) spans. Nearby St. George's Hall was once, in Victorian days, the home of political and musical Bradford. It faces Britannia House, a modern business block with a copper dome. Not far away is the **Bradford Playhouse**, formerly known as the 'Civic', the best known amateur theatre in the North of England, and in Denholme, Blackfoot Mill testifies that this is a city with its feet on the ground.

Bradford Town Hall, built last century and based on a building in Florence, is one of the city's **most striking buildings**. It has an imposing facade, resplendent with a tower, fine windows, open parapets, gables and a splendid sculpture gallery of Kings and Queens. The entrance is charming, while inside, among the scores of rooms, the superb banqueting hall has windows aglow with shields and walls hung with pictures. Near to it is another fine building, the **Exchange,** with its tower and a slender spire 45 metres (150 ft) high. Then there is Commerce House, headquarters of the Chamber of Commerce, which is matched by the Post Office, a handsome building built in 1887 in the Italian style. The College of Art, in Great Horton Road, is near the new University which has the right to grant its own degrees. In 1824 the Royal Infirmary was established on a 9 hectare (23 acre) site on Daisy Hill.

Lister **Park** and Bowling Park are on opposite sides of the city, each with more than 20 hectares (50 acres). Bradford Moor Park and Horton Park lie east and west while Peel Park, the largest comprising 22 hectares (56 acres), lies east of Lister Park. Should you wish to lose the sight of the industrial world altogether, the place to be is **Baildon Moor**, just 3 miles (5 kms) north of the city centre. There, within its 300 hectares (750 acres) the fresh air you breath is blowing at a height of 275 metres (900 ft) above sea level.

Lister Park is a delight. It has lawns, flowers, trees, spacious drives and **the biggest Botanical Gardens outside London**. There is a splendid pool, a boating lake and shady walks, all of which combine to make a noble setting for Bradford's Art Gallery and Museum, which is housed in the Cartwright Memorial Hall. It is largely to Edmund Cartwright's inventions that Bradford owes its prosperity. The Hall is also a tribute to Samuel Cunliffe Lister, the first Lord Masham, who founded the Manningham Silk Mills.

There is a fine collection of model trams in classical **Cartwright Hall**, which also houses many art treasures and collections of natural history and archaeology. Many of the paintings are of the British School and include many pictures by Yorkshire artists.

Bolling Park, with its sloping lawns and, in season, rhododendrons, overlooks the city. Facing it are four broad flights of steps climbing to the terraced gardens of Bolling Hall, a lovely old house with two towers. It is one of Bradford's links with days gone by and is now **a Museum** illustrating the history of the city, its neighbourhood and the condition of life since the C14th when the old house was being built. Down the centuries it has been the home of the Bollings, the Tempests, the Windleys and the Woods; and along the years it has been extended to such a degree that a tour of its rooms is a journey down five centuries. However, its glory declined until it was divided into tenements. Today, **splendid restoration** has transformed it into a fascinating building.

BRADFORD CITY CENTRE ATTRACTIONS

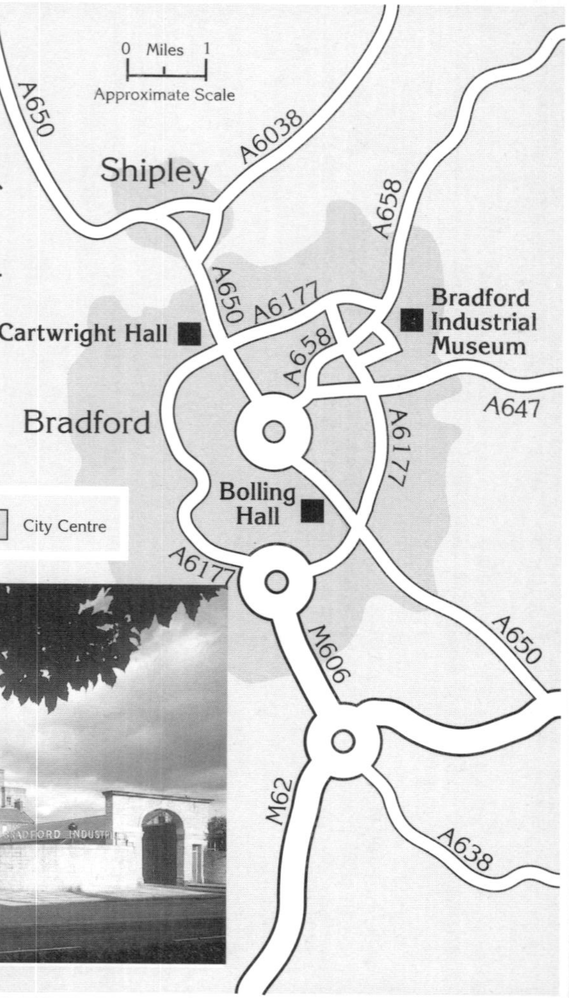

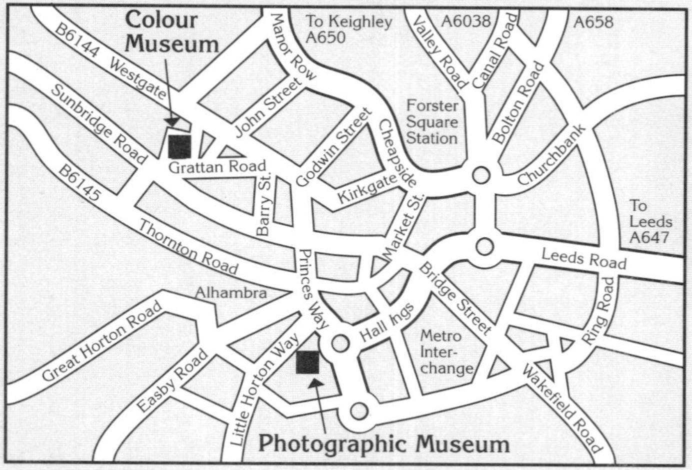

The oldest part of the house is the **south west tower,** which is believed to have been built by Robert Bolling **six hundred years ago.** The chimney stack and the arch of the fireplace are Tudor and the rest of the house, including a second tower, is early C17th. The drawing room by the medieval tower was panelled and its beautiful fireplace installed about 1700 and the wing by the new tower was modelled in Adam style after a fire in the C18th.

The **medieval tower** contains some C15th and C17th chests and a C18th fire engine. The oak rafters and the low fireplace of the Tudor kitchen give it an added attractiveness, while in the pantry there are some wooden churns and grain measures, man traps, a box mangle and a flail for threshing corn.

Those rooms modelled in the Adam style are noted for their plaster ceilings, cornices and woodwork. They contain **collections** of swords, rapiers, daggers, watchman's rattles, musical instruments, brass, copper and pewter ware and many other fascinating items. Elsewhere there are fine examples of English glass and earthenware. In fact the whole house is a rich treasure-house of which Bradford is justifiably proud.

Bradford also takes pride in honouring its benefactors. The list is long and glorious and includes **Lord Masham** and **Sir Titus Salt,** whose effigies stand in Lister Park. **Robert Peel** is in Peel Place and **William Edward Forster,** who made **education** the birthright of every child, is in a square named after him. **Richard Oastler**, in Darley Street, was the man who fought to reduce the hours worked by children in the mills.

While Bradford honours its outstanding sons, its commoner men, who gave their lives that others might live in peace, are not forgotten. All are commemorated in **an imposing cenotaph** bearing bronze figures of a soldier and a sailor.

Sir Henry Irving made his last stage appearance at Bradford's Theatre Royal, dying in his hotel shortly afterwards, within an hour of speaking his last words 'Into thy hands, O Lord, Into thy Hands'.

The city's **roll of honour** is long and covers a broad spectrum: **John Cousen**, the brilliant engraver of Turner's pictures; **John Sharp,** Archbishop of York when Anne was Queen; and **John Fawcett,** the C18th hymn writer.

Fredrick Delius was born in a house near the Technical College in 1863. The house was demolished to make way for a garage but the music of Delius, through which he expresses the glory of the English countryside, is immortal. **Sir Frank Dyson,** Astronomer Royal, was educated at Bradford Grammar School. **Sir Douglas Mawson**, the last Antarctic explorer, who sailed with Shackleton in 1908, was born in Bradford in 1882. The novelist and playwright **J B Priestley**, who was born in Bradford in 1894, unwittingly summarises these remarkable people in the title of his first successful novel, published in 1929, 'The Good Companions'.

Bradford achieved city status in 1920 when the **parish church of Saint Peter** became **a Cathedral.** It stands, a noble pile, on a steep hillside on the site of a church believed to have been Saxon. Built into a wall on the north side of the Cathedral is a stone carved with knotwork that is pre-Norman Conquest. The chancel and the clerestoried nave are mainly C14th but the west bay of the nave was added when the tower was built in the C15th. Most of the windows are medieval and the Bowling Chapel is about 500 years old. The splendid spire-shaped cover to the modern font is C15th. There are some old moulded beams in the roofs and twenty angels carry the nave roof with its traceried gables and richly coloured bosses shining with gold. Linenfold panelling enriches the bishop's throne.

The cathedral contains a monument to the memory of another famous son of Bradford, **Joseph Priestley**, the civil engineer, who died in 1817. The monument carries a carving of the Leeds to Liverpool Canal.

There are **many modern churches** in Bradford, one of which, St. Oswald's, has a high tower with a spire which contains dormer windows. It is built in the C14th style, is spacious and has arches running from east to west. The font is richly carved with tracery and leaves. The head of the Lord, surrounded by angels, is seen in the tracery in the east window. At the base of the window are tiny pictures of the Virgin Mary, with the boy Jesus, and the Crucifixion.

From such rich skeins has this ancient wool town been woven, to become a proud city with a glorious history that has diversified to meet the needs of modern day England.

Whilst touring in the South Pennines area the visitor will find a visit to **Leeds** a rewarding experience. Leeds is the regional capital of Yorkshire and the **third largest city in England**, with all the attributes which such a description leads the visitor to expect. As befits a town that took pride in its growth during the C19th to become the world leader in the production of cloth, it has Victorian buildings - the Town Hall, Park Square, the Institute, the Arcades - that reflect the prosperity of those days. But it is also a city with modern facilities, festive, cultural and sporting occasions, and the will, to suit all tastes; truly a City of Varieties.

Leeds itself is **one of the greenest cities in Europe**, with more parks than any major British conurbation; it is the prettiest floral city in Yorkshire, brimming with fine parklands, countryside trails and plantsmens' gardens, whilst the countryside round about is full of a wide range of botanical showpieces, from the Japanese Garden in **Horsforth Hall Park** to the ponds and cascades in the French style to be found in the Pleasure Gardens of **Bramham Park. Roundhay Park** alone can provide a varied feast for the senses, with a Tropical World of plants, insects, butterflies and fish, together with a more homely century-old rose garden, a wood, canal gardens, a lake and a scented garden for the blind. **Golden Acre Park,** too, boasts a lake, with exotic wildfowl, amongst more than 40 hectares (100 acres) of woods and gardens; and one of the finest collections of exotic birds, many of endangered species, in the country can be seen among the ornamental gardens at **Lotherton.** Within the extensive parkland and woodland of **Temple Newsam House** is Home Farm, at which many of the cattle, sheep and goats are rare breeds.

Leeds' **cultural, historical and architectural heritage** are abundantly reflected in its wealth of museums and art galleries, and its Stately Homes, many of which are also employed to exhibit relics of the past and works of art. The industrial past of Leeds and the South Pennines is exhibited at the award-winning **Armley Mills Industrial Museum**, which shows the development of the major local industries. This is neatly balanced by a visit to the **Kirkstall Abbey House Folk Museum** with its reconstructed Victorian streets which concentrates upon the changing day to day lives of ordinary people **The City Museum** is more cosmopolitan, with collections of artefacts from all over the world. **Leeds City Art Gallery** focuses the attention on C19th and C20th British, French and American art, whilst the **Henry Moore Sculpture Gallery and Centre** has a comprehensive range of sculpture on exhibition.

The revitalised **waterfront** area in the city centre, and the **Middleton Steam Railway** (which, dated at 1758, has claims to be the oldest in the world) also offer revelations of the city's past history.

There are **four major stately homes** not far to the east of Leeds. **Harewood House** has a display of furniture, paintings and porcelain inside its palatial buildings and outside in the landscaped Capability Brown gardens there is a Bird Garden and an Adventure Playground. Similar displays may be found at **Bramham Park**, a Queen Anne mansion; **Temple Newsam Estate**, a Tudor-Jacobean house containing the Chippendale furniture collection among other important exhibits; and at the more recently-constructed **Lotherton Hall,** which has in addition Chinese ceramics and a costume and fashion exhibition.

Theatrical experiences in buildings old and new are on offer to the theatre lover in Leeds. **The Grand Theatre**, based on La Scala, Milan and recently restored, has celebrity performances and three seasons of drama, dance and music. By contrast the new **West Yorkshire Playhouse** offers five different performance spaces and performances to take advantage of their flexibility. **The Civic Theatre** is home to the city's leading amateur operatic and dramatic societies as well as having a varied programme of professional work. Possibly best-known, through its television exposure in 'The Good Old Days', is the **City Varieties Theatre**, which shrugs off its Victorian image when the TV cameras aren't there, and stages very modern jazz, folk and rock concerts!

Dance, too, has an enthusiastic following in Leeds. The **Yorkshire Dance Centre** is flourishing, with its many classes, and housing the professional Phoenix Dance Company. The **Northern School of Contemporary Dance** also provides an opportunity to see high-quality dance in many forms in the City.

Symphony Concerts are held at the Town Hall, and the City is, of course, known the

LEEDS CITY ATTRACTIONS

1. Central Bus Station
2. Metro WYMTA
3. Vicar Lane Bus Station
4. Wellington Street Coach Station-National Express
5. Yorkshire Rider Offices
6. Bond Street Centre
7. Corn Exchange
8. Granary Wharfe
9. Kirkgate Market
10. Merrion Centre
11. Schofield Centre
12. St John's Centre
13. Cannon Cinema
14. City Varieties
15. Civic Theatre
16. Grand Theatre
17. Leeds Playhouse
18. Odeon Cinema
19. West Yorkshire Playhouse
20. Art Gallery
21. Henry Moore Gallery
22. Polytechnic Gallery
23. The Art Company
24. University Gallery
25. BBC TV Studios
26. City Treasury
27. Civic Hall
28. Holy Trinity Church
29. Leeds Methodist Mission-(Oxford Place Centre)
30. Leeds Parish Church
31. Library
32. Mill Hill Chapel
33. Museum
34. St. Anne's Cathedral
35. St. Georges Church and Crypt
36. St. John's Church (redundant)
37. Tourist Information Centre
38. Town Hall
39. Westgate International Swimming Pool

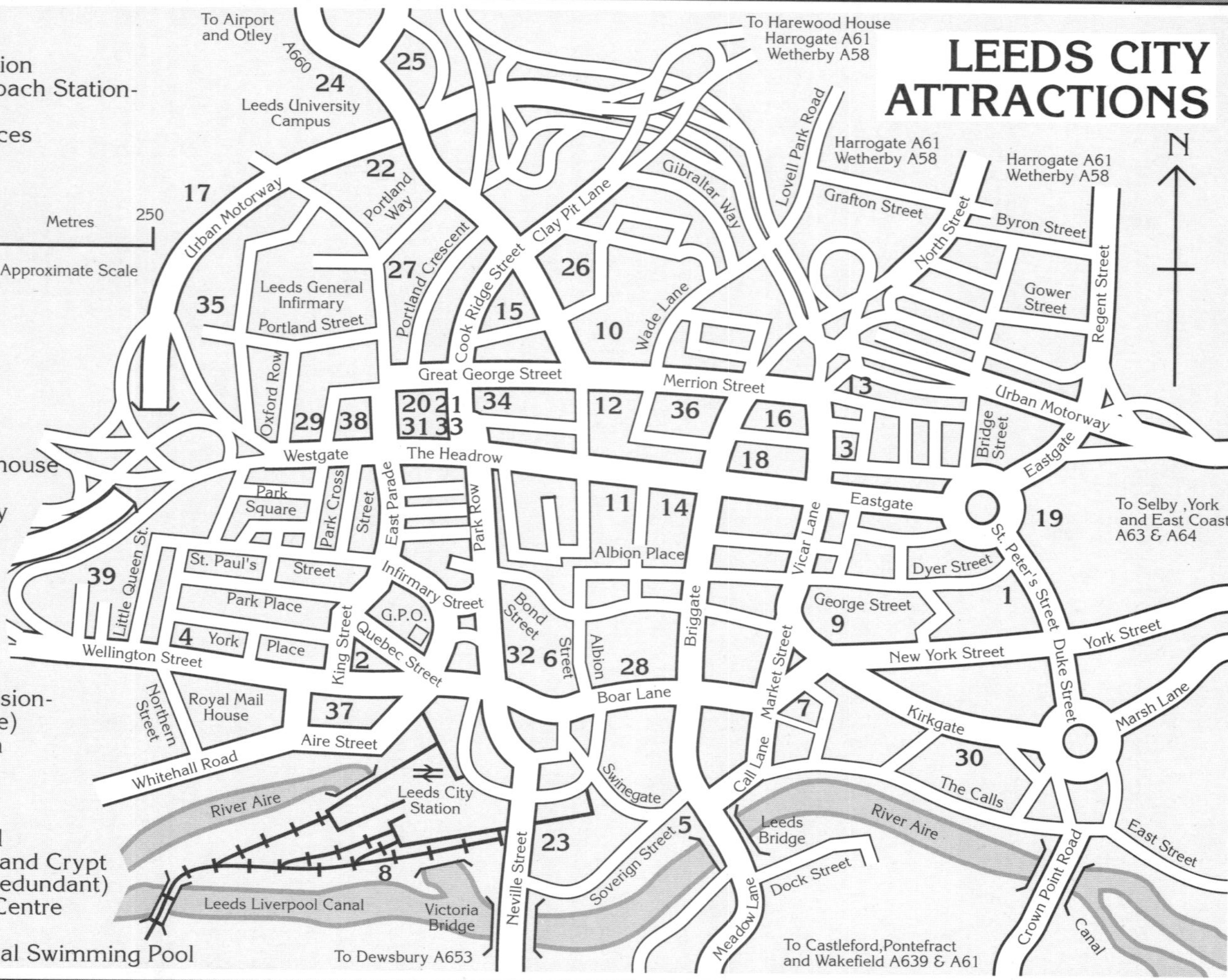

world over for its **Leeds International Piano Competition.** The International Concert Season provides 150 concerts from October to June.

Opera North also has its home in Leeds, based on the **Grand Theatre**. Throughout the year there is a lively and wide choice of music around the city, from lunchtime orchestral concerts, to brass bands in the parks to the high class events of Leeds Jazz, to open-air rock concerts at Roundhay Park. There are two independent cinemas in the city, and the **Leeds International Film Festival** is held each October.

The arts combine in lively fashion every August Bank Holiday in the increasingly popular **Leeds West Indian Carnival Parade**, the biggest in the UK outside London.

Whatever the sporting requirements of the visitor - as spectator or participant, novice or expert - Leeds has an abundance of **sporting opportunities** to offer, with its 22 leisure and recreational centres throughout the City, and professional facilities and teams to match any. The Recreation Department claim that every sport can be enjoyed in Leeds.

The **Headingly** cricket ground is well-known wherever cricket is played, as the headquarters of Yorkshire and the stage of many a famous Test Match. **Elland Road,** equally, has a household ring to it, probably from the heady days of the Revie era, when Leeds United stood second to none, a glory which may even now be returning. Rugby Football is also strongly represented in the city, with four amateur Union teams and three professional League sides. (Incidentally, for Rugby League fans, **The Rugby League Hall of Fame**, with RL memorabilia, is at the Bentley Arms, Oulton).

For those more disposed to taking part in less violent activities, the area is well served by a range of some **seventeen swimming pools** and **twenty-one golf courses**. The city is currently making a claim to be the premier swimming city in the country and has, at the top of its range, the Leeds International Pool, but the leisure pools offer lessons and supervised swimming sessions for less ambitious swimmers. There are five municipal golf courses, Roundhay, Middleton, Gotts Park and Temple Newsam (2), with sixteen indoor driving bays at Oulton Driving Range. Meanwhile, Ripon, Wetherby and York are the nearest racecourses.

Leeds is a veritable **Mecca for shoppers** - many northern bus companies put on Leeds Shopping Excursions in the run up to Christmas, for example. There is one of the largest pedestrian precincts in Europe, so that traffic-free streets give easy access to the shops, within a compact shopping area. Briggate bustles with the expected major high street stores, whilst bargain-hunters will not beat the famous Kirkgate Market. **Victorian covered arcades** - Thornton's, Queens, County, Central, Victoria and Grand - form a superb network of fascinating shops and architectural features and there are four modern indoor shopping centres, with the reconstructed Corn Exchange being the latest addition to the variety of shopping available. At the Leeds Canal Basin, near the main Railway Station, is **Granary Wharf**, the venue for a new centre for craftsmen and women to make and sell their work, with indoor shops and an outdoor market.

There are many **open markets** in towns in the area - Wetherby, Otley, Morley and Pudsey - as well as the Leeds Open Market, and the abundant Mill Shops are becoming very popular bargain-sources with tourists as well as local people.

City centre pubs and wine bars are numerous, catering for a wide range of tastes from the slick Observatory with its transatlantic gleaming chrome to Leeds' oldest inn, Whitelocks, serving traditional Yorkshire food in its Victorian decor of glazed tiles and stained glass. Real ale aficionados will really relish a visit to the Adelphi whilst the Bingley Arms at Bardsey, featured in the Guinness Book of Records as England's oldest inn, provides dining out in a rural setting. The City's **restaurants** offer a cosmopolitan feast - Chinese, French, Italian, Indian, Vegetarian - something to suit everyone. The city is well-provided with Night-clubs and Discotheques.

A short distance from Leeds the visitor can explore the **glorious rolling countryside** of Lower Wharfedale with its riverside market towns of Otley and Wetherby. There are many nature reserves and country parks, chief of which is Otley Chevin Forest Park, 283 hectares (700 acres) of open moorland, forest, crags and panoramic views. Equally splendid for walking is the 9 mile (14 km) Meanwood Valley Trail, linking Woodhouse Moor with Golden Acre Park. Finally, The West Yorkshire Cycle Route offers similar attractions for cyclists.

Most of the following museums are open regularly, at least during the tourist season. If you are making a special journey, however, please be sure to check with a TIC beforehand, to avoid possible disappointment.

Please note that the district in which each museum is located is given in brackets after the location.

ABBEY HOUSE MUSEUM Kirkstall Abbey (Leeds). This attractive old building was the gatehouse to the Abbey and you might expect to find the Abbey's history depicted therein. If so, you are in for a surprise, because the museum is in fact crammed with everything used and enjoyed by the people of Leeds from the mid C18th onwards. There are three reconstructed Victorian streets full of shops and small houses, their interiors perfect in every detail - and the collections of period toys are outstanding.

ARMLEY MILLS INDUSTRIAL MUSEUM Leeds. This award winning museum occupies what was once the largest woollen mill in the world. It comes to life especially at weekends, when the machinery can be seen in action, demonstrating all the stages of the clothing industry - but it is fascinating at any time, containing other displays on the history of the moving image, the electrification of the City and the history of haulage under ground.

AUTOMOBILIA Hebden Bridge (Calderdale). Nostalgia for the age of 'motoring' (all we do these days, alas, is 'drive'!) will take you to this delightful museum, where there is a fine array of Austin 7s, Morris cars, old motorcycles and motoring memorabilia.

BACUP NATURAL HISTORY MUSEUM Bacup (Rossendale). The museum contains a vast collection of photographs of natural history, as well as items portraying the domestic life and industry of recent centuries in this area.

BAGSHAW MUSEUM Batley (Kirklees). This unusual monster of a Victorian house, once the home of a local mill-owner, now contains an interesting local, natural history and Oriental collection.

BANCROFT MILL ENGINE MUSEUM Barnoldswick (Oldham). The engine was part of the last cotton weaving shed to be built in Barnoldswick in 1920. The mill closed in 1978 but the engine was reprieved and restored. The 36 metre (120 foot) chimney was also preserved as a notable local landmark, along with the boilers.

BANKFIELD MUSEUM AND GALLERY Halifax (Calderdale). The exceptional series of temporary exhibitions held here makes the Gallery worth a visit at any time - but the Museum more than holds its own too, containing natural history exhibits and the best collection of textiles and costume in the area. It is an Italianate palazzo, built for a C19th mill owner, Edward Akroyd, and sited in beautiful grounds on a hill overlooking Halifax. Also at Bankfield is the Duke of Wellington's Regimental Museum.

BATLEY ART GALLERY Batley (Kirklees). Regular temporary exhibitions make it well worth keeping an eye on this gallery.

BLAKEY LOCK, KEY AND SAFE MUSEUM Brierfield, Lancashire (Pendle). Housed in the Blakey Lock Works, this unusual collection is open by arrangement. Exhibits include a fascinating collection of locks and keys, some dating back as early as Roman times.

BRACKEN HALL COUNTRYSIDE CENTRE Baildon, Shipley (Bradford). The famously beautiful Shipley Glen is the location for this attraction, where displays feature the geology, wildlife and history of the area. Regular special events are held.

BRADFORD INDUSTRIAL MUSEUM Moorside Road (Bradford). See special feature under 'Bradford's Museums'. This former spinning mill shows all the stages from raw wool to finished cloth, with working textile machinery, transport gallery and furnished mill manager's house, bistro and mill shop.

BRITISH IN INDIA MUSEUM Colne (Pendle). A fascinating collection of memorabilia relating to the period of the British Raj, featuring paintings, coins, medals, photographs, documents and models - including a working model of the Kalka-Simla Railway.

BRONTË PARSONAGE MUSEUM Haworth (Bradford). This Georgian building was built in 1777 and the Brontë family moved there in 1820. Patrick Brontë died there in 1861 after more than forty years as the local incumbent. As a result, there are numerous personal relics of the Brontës, though little of their own actual furniture - so suitable furniture of the period has been used. Copies of wallpaper found among Charlotte's personal possessions have been hung on the walls and a permanent exhibition, 'The Brontës - A Family History' fills in the story most effectively. Controversial plans for a new museum are under discussion and these point up a problem, namely that there are so many visitors - so do go on a weekday if you can.

BRONTË WEAVING SHED Haworth (Bradford). Here you can see genuine Yorkshire tweed, still being produced as it was a century ago, in a restored weaving shed. There is a display about the last Yorkshire handloom weaver, 'Owld Timmy Feather', authentic looms and, if you feel inclined, the chance to have a go for yourself and discover that weaving really was an art - the machine by no means did it all!

BURNLEY MECHANICS ARTS AND ENTERTAINMENT CENTRE Not exactly a museum, but well worth seeking out for one of the liveliest programmes of music, drama, arts, crafts workshops and other events you are likely to find anywhere.

BYGONE DAYS MUSEUM OF MEMORABILIA Haworth (Bradford) see under 'Haworth Village' in 'Stately Homes and Other Historic Sites.'

CALDERDALE INDUSTRIAL MUSEUM Halifax (Calderdale). You are warmly invited to visit this Museum adjacent to the marvellous Piece Hall and 'clock in' to experience the sights, sounds and smells of our industrial past. Among the 100 working exhibits are examples of textile machines and steam engines, along with special displays on old Halifax and the Luddites. See special feature elsewhere in this guide.

CANAL AND COUNTRYSIDE CENTRE Tunnel End, Marsden (Kirklees). Housed in the former canal keeper's cottage is this small museum and countryside interpretation centre. The Kirklees Countryside Unit operates a programme of guided walks and other activities from here. For further details of the Canal's history see the chapter 'Transport by Water - The Canals.'

CANNON HILL COUNTRY PARK AND MUSEUM Denby Dale (Kirklees). Housed in a fine C18th Hall, this museum features local history and natural history and includes a military section.

CARTWRIGHT HALL ART GALLERY Bradford (Bradford). See special feature under 'Bradford's Museums.' This superb building in the Baroque style houses varied and changing art exhibitions, aimed at reflecting the richness of Bradford's cultural mix. The permanent collections include work by pre-Raphaelite painters such as Dante Gabriel Rossetti and Ford Madox Brown, and continue through the Victorian period to the present day, featuring work by David Hockney, among many others.

CHILDHOOD REFLECTIONS Hebden Bridge (Calderdale). This is what its subtitle says, a Museum of Dolls, Toys and Miniatures. Meccano enthusiasts will be delighted to find working Meccano models - and if you really want to wallow in nostalgia, there is a shop selling old cars, trains, dolls and other toys. Tea, coffee and snacks are available.

CITY MUSEUM Leeds. The City Museum has been open for over 150 years, displaying a fantastic wealth of collections from all over the world. Here you will find dinosaurs, an Egyptian mummy, examples of Greek and Roman sculpture, coins, costumes and an especially fine collection of natural history specimens, including an alarmingly lifelike Bengal tiger and, believe it or not, the largest egg on earth!

CLIFFE CASTLE MUSEUM AND ART GALLERY Keighley (Bradford). Formerly the home of Henry Isaac Butterfield, this fine house is furnished in the style of 1886, the peak of Victorian prosperity. Features include the Airedale Gallery and a display entitled 'Molecule to Minerals' - as well as interesting temporary exhibitions. There's plenty to do outside too, with beautiful grounds, a bird garden, cactus house and flower garden.

COLNE VALLEY MUSEUM Golcar (Kirklees). This Museum is situated in Golcar, a former weaving community where there are many fine examples of weavers' cottages, with their long rows of mullioned windows. The Museum is set in a group of cottages and includes the loom chamber, living room and kitchen of the domestic weaver, as well as a gas-lit clogger's shop. Spinning, weaving and other crafts are demonstrated. See special feature elsewhere in this guide.

COLOUR MUSEUM Bradford (Bradford). Step into the fascinating world of colour. Why is it so important? How do we use it? Britain's only Museum of Colour answers these questions and many more - see special feature elsewhere in this guide.

DEWSBURY MUSEUM Dewsbury (Kirklees). Here the concentration is on the theme of Childhood, with delightful displays evoking the world of the nursery from the C18th onwards.

EARBY LEAD MINES Earby (Pendle). This small museum is full of fascination. Housed in a former, early C17th Grammar School, it tells the story of C19th lead mining in the Yorkshire Dales, an important chapter in the area's industrial history which has disappeared almost entirely from view but which is not forgotten.

EASTTHORPE GALLERY Mirfield (Kirklees). Here there is a regular programme of changing exhibitions, mainly featuring contemporary art and design, open to the public, as well as workshop tuition available to members.

ELLENROAD MILL ENGINE Ellenroad (Rochdale). The Ellenroad Trust have worked hard and long to restore to its original working condition this site. It is, in fact, the largest and most complete spinning mill beam engine complex surviving in Britain today, and does much to explain and re-create the lifestyle and working atmosphere of the period.

GREATER MANCHESTER FIRE SERVICE MUSEUM (Rochdale). This Museum traces the story of fire fighting, from the earliest fire engines to the present day. Among the beautifully presented exhibits are 11 gleaming fire engines, street and Blitz scenes, and a wealth of memorabilia.

HEBBLE END WORKS Hebden Bridge (Calderdale). The historic buildings here have been cleverly and sensitively converted to provide a crafts workplace where visitors can watch artists and craftspeople at work and, if they choose, buy some treasure to take home. As a demonstration of traditional skills, it is, if you like, a living museum. Particularly popular with children is the ever fascinating 'World of the Honey Bee', a live exhibition in which the bees can be safely observed, while talks and videos explain the honey-making process.

THE HEBDEN CRYPT Hebden Bridge (Calderdale). If you enjoy having your nerves jangled, this is the one for you - but do be warned, because the sensibilities are not spared; the full horror of the darker sides of man's personality are explored, with scenes from both reality and legend depicted in all their gory glory! It is meant to frighten - and it does - but it is informative too, as an exploration of some of man's most villainous crimes and most sinister imaginings.

HELMSHORE TEXTILE MUSEUMS Helmshore (Rossendale). Working textile machinery is on view here, in two restored cotton mills.

HOLMFIRTH POSTCARD MUSEUM Holmfirth (Kirklees). Nothing could contrast more with the previous entry than this, perhaps the most frivolous museum in the country! It is a serious museum too, however, the only one in the UK devoted to the history of postcards. It is based on the local firm of Bamforth's, pioneers of silent films and saucy seaside postcards. The vast, amazing collection on display here includes cards from the Scherer Collection of 30,000 cards given to Kirklees Council by the ex-curator of the National Philatelic Museum in the USA. There are postcard galleries, silent films and a video re-enactment of the great Holmfirth flood of 1852 (see under 'Holmfirth' in 'Cotton and Wool: Towns and Villages').

HORSES AT WORK Halifax (Calderdale). This, the National Museum of the Working Horse, is a very special place for all who love horses and experience certain longings for the agricultural past as it used to be. Not only are there exhibitions about working horses, with tack, horse drawn machinery, vehicles and photographs - there are also the horses themselves, still being trained in the old-fashioned way and ready to give waggon rides to visitors young and old. As well as the Stable Museum, there is a Pets' Corner, Picnic Area and refreshments available from the 'Carter's Rest.'

HUDDERSFIELD ART GALLERY Huddersfield (Kirklees). Here you can look back over a century of art in Britain, picking out works by such artists as Graham Sutherland, Henry Moore, L.S. Lowry and Francis Bacon. There are also small collections of English watercolours and Japanese prints. The contemporary theme is continued in a year round programme of temporary exhibitions.

JOSEPH DOBSON AND SONS LTD. Elland (Calderdale). They started in 1850 and they have been making the famous boiled sweets ever since - but you need to come in an organised party and book in advance if you want to see how it's done.

KEIGHLEY AND WORTH VALLEY RAILWAY Oxenhope (Bradford). A living Museum, used for the film of 'The Railway Children' and some 'Sherlock Holmes' episodes, where historic steam engines and carriages are lovingly maintained to take visitors on the only 'Complete Branch Line Railway.' The Railway's own Museum is at Oxenhope, and there is a Carriage Museum at Ingrow West. Haworth, in addition to its own many attractions, has the Railway Bookshop, while Damems is the smallest British Station. Souvenirs and refreshments are available at the two ends of the line, Keighley and Oxenhope. See also 'Stately Homes and Other Historic Sites.'

MUSEUM OF LEEDS Leeds. This open air museum consists of canalside footpath trail, along the valley of the River Aire, which connects some forty sites of historic interest, including the Armley Mills (see above) and Kirkstall Abbey (see 'Stately Homes and Other Historic Sites') - an imaginative approach which won it the Industrial Museum of the Year award in 1983.

NATIONAL MUSEUM OF PHOTOGRAPHY, FILM AND TELEVISION (Bradford). See special feature elsewhere in this guide. Housing the 19 metre (62 foot) wide giant IMAX, Britain's largest cinema screen, the Museum's other galleries cover the history of photography, news photography and imaging, along with electronic images from microbiology and weather satellites.

PENDLE HERITAGE CENTRE Nelson, Lancashire. This is a regional Centre for Heritage Education and Interpretation, housing both permanent displays and changing exhibitions about traditional buildings and conservation projects in the area.

PETER BLACK CAR COLLECTION Keighley (Bradford). If you adore vintage cars and are fascinated by motoring memorabilia, you will love this collection of 100 vehicles going back very nearly 100 years - but you have to make an appointment to see them.

PIECE HALL Halifax (Calderdale). Explore the colonnades and cobbled courtyard of this magnificent C18th cloth hall. The Museum features the period to which this mighty building belongs, the Pre-Industrial Age of cloth manufacture in Calderdale. Meanwhile, on the so-called 'Rustic' level, you will usually find a fascinating exhibition of contemporary art or craft, often with the artists and craftspeople actually at work. The Central Courtyard is a perfect amphitheatre for a whole host of entertainments, from full-scale concerts to dancers and jugglers. See 'Stately Homes and Other Historic Sites.'

QUEEN STREET MILL MUSEUM (Burnley) see 'Stately Homes and Other Historic Sites.'

RED HOUSE MUSEUM Gomersal (Kirklees). This delightful C17th house, with its Brontë and Wesleyan connections, houses furnishings and other items from the 1820s. There is also a charming garden, currently being restored.

ROCHDALE MUSEUM (Rochdale). This interesting local history Museum tells the story of Rochdale from fossils to clogs, giving an insight into the lives of ordinary people - and some less ordinary ones, like John Bright and Gracie Fields.

ROCHDALE PIONEERS CO-OPERATIVE MUSEUM (Rochdale). The Co-operative Movement, which has spread world wide, had its origins here, where the original shop, opened in 1844, still stands in the middle of a conservation area and tells the story of the Movement from its very earliest beginnings on to the present day.

ROCK WATER BIRD CONSERVATION CENTRE Cliviger (Burnley). Breeding of common and endangered species is carried out here, in spacious and picturesque surroundings. Tours and talks are available.

ROSSENDALE MUSEUM Rawtenstall (Rossendale). A former mill owner's mansion, this Museum is sited in the delightful Whitaker Park, Rawtenstall. It houses several collections of local interest, fine and decorative arts, natural history and temporary exhibitions.

RYBURN FARM MUSEUM Ripponden (Calderdale). All the atmosphere of a traditional C19th Pennine hill farm is captured in this small farmhouse, with its cosy kitchen, dairy, loom chamber and collection of farming bygones.

SADDLEWORTH MUSEUM Uppermill (Oldham). Once a woollen mill, its exhibits include a full-sized, furnished reconstruction of a C19th clothier's cottage and a working woollen mill gallery.

SALTAIRE MUSEUM OF VICTORIAN REED ORGANS AND HARMONIUMS Saltaire (Bradford). Phil and Pam Fluke invite enthusiasts to see their remarkable private collection and try them out if they are organists themselves.

SHIBDEN HALL FOLK MUSEUM Halifax (Calderdale). In this peaceful setting (see also 'Stately Homes and Other Historic Sites') is a Museum of domestic life, with period rooms and a C19th village. Boating lake and miniature railway.

SMITH ART GALLERY Brighouse (Calderdale). This formal, classical C19th mansion houses temporary exhibitions, some from its own collections and others on tour.

TOLSON MUSEUM Huddersfield (Kirklees). Housed in an Italianate Victorian mansion, the Museum features fine collections of local history, toys, transport, glassware, silver and natural history. There are relics of the area's architectural heritage in the grounds of the Museum.

TOWNELEY HALL ART GALLERY, MUSEUM, MUSEUM OF LOCAL CRAFTS & INDUSTRIES and NATURAL HISTORY CENTRE Burnley. Dating from the C14th, this historic house, with rooms furnished in period, houses both permanent and travelling exhibitions. The numerous features of interest include an historic Ice House in the grounds.

WORLD OF SOOTY Bradford. Trace the TV character's rise to stardom through the sets, props, scripts and photos which have enthralled the very young and the very old for 35 years.

YORKSHIRE MINING MUSEUM Caphouse Colliery (Kirklees). Here you can experience life at the coal face, seeing life-size figures in a re-creation of the working life and conditions of coal miners from the C18th right up to the modern mine, with its giant excavating machines. See special feature elsewhere in this guide.

The properties in the following list are mostly open daily in season but, if you are making a special journey, do please check through a TIC beforehand, to avoid possible disappointment.

The letters NT indicate the National Trust. The district in which each property is found is given in brackets after the location.

BOLLING HALL Bowling Hall Road, Bradford (Bradford). This interesting building displays a range of architectural styles, beginning with the mid C15th pele tower and ending with the late C18th wing designed by John Carr of York. Carr's drawing room is especially fine and the so-called Ghost Room, has a remarkable ceiling. The rooms are furnished to fit their respective periods. There is also a local history collection.

BRONTË PARSONAGE Haworth (Bradford). This, one of the most visited houses in Britain, is a somewhat austere building in Georgian style surrounded by a neat garden. It contains many mementoes of the famous Brontë family, including some original furniture, items of clothing and examples of their writings and drawings. See also the entry under 'Museums.'

CASTLE HILL JUBILEE TOWER Huddersfield (Kirklees). The Jubilee in question was Queen Victoria's, in 1898, and the tower, which is impressive if not exactly beautiful, surveys a site which has been occupied since the earliest times. Men came here in the Stone Age, built a fort, whose ramparts can still be seen in the Iron Age, and in the C12th converted it into a castle - and this remarkable story is told in the exhibition inside the Tower.

CASTLESHAW ROMAN FORT Delph (Oldham). High above Delph, excavations have unearthed the foundations of a Roman Fort built on the old military road from Chester to York. Some of its banks and ditches have now been reconstructed.

CLIFFE CASTLE See under 'Museums.'

DELPH and DOBCROSS (Oldham). These two fine villages in the heart of Saddleworth hold great charm. The village square and weavers' cottages of Dobcross and the craft shops, antiques and country pubs of Delph are linked by a walk along the old Delph-Donley railway line.

EAST RIDDLESDEN HALL (NT) Keighley (Bradford). This excellent old manor house was restored in the early 1980s and now presents an interior typical of a wealthy West Yorkshire landowner in the C17th. There is wood panelling in the main rooms, fine plasterwork, oak furniture and a collection of pewter. The stone flagged kitchen appeals to many visitors. The whole is complemented by a splendid medieval tithe barn, set in an attractive formal garden and grounds. Other attractions include the exhibition, the Bothy Tearoom and shop.

GAWTHORPE HALL (NT) Padiham (Burnley). An early C17th manor house with fine panelling, moulded ceilings and a Jacobean long gallery. It is the home of the Rachel Kay Shuttleworth collections of costumes, embroidery, lace and woven textiles. There is also the Ryder collection of early English and European furniture, several fine paintings and other objets d'art. The Estate Building has been restored to offer estate management, crafts and other courses. There is also an attractive garden and a shop.

GOODSHAW OLD BAPTIST CHURCH Goodshaw (Rossendale). A celebrated group of local musicians, known as the 'Larks of Dean', used this chapel, built in 1760, as their base. They wrote a number of well known and very popular hymns.

HAREWOOD HOUSE AND BIRD GARDEN north of Leeds. Though on the edges of the area covered by this guide, this lovely C18th house, the home of the Lascelles family (the Earl of Harewood), certainly deserves a visit. It was designed by John Carr of York in 1759, with interior decoration by Robert Adam. It contains Chippendale furniture, fine paintings and superb collections of French and Oriental porcelain. The grounds were landscaped by 'Capability' Brown and now also contain a Bird Garden, which is the place to see a whole range of exotic species. Restaurant, cafeteria, shops and adventure playground.

HARRY RAMSDEN'S White Cross, Guiseley (Leeds). Hardly an historic building but certainly a traditional part of Yorkshire life, this is said to be the largest - and probably most comfortable - fish and chip shop in the world!

HAWORTH VILLAGE (Bradford). This famous village deserves a visit in its own right, not simply for the Brontë Parsonage. It is said to be haunted by the tragic Brontës and, apart from the Parsonage, the principal places to visit are the Church, where the Reverend Patrick Brontë preached, and the Black Bull Inn, where his unfortunate son, Branwell, drank himself to oblivion. Bygone Days, in Belle Isle Road, has a rather quaint facade giving access to a courtyard of shops and a small museum of memorabilia, in which many items from various television productions, such as 'Last of the Summer Wine', 'Rising Damp' and 'In Loving Memory' are displayed. It is very close to Haworth Station, on the Keighley and Worth Valley Railway line, also a star of the silver screen (see below). All around Haworth, meanwhile, lie the moors on which the Brontë children roamed and which form the setting for Charlotte's 'Jane Eyre', Emily's 'Wuthering Heights' and Anne's 'The Tenant of Wildfell Hall' - and if you can't find their ghosts in the now very tourist conscious village, you will surely find them here.

HEPTONSTALL GRAMMAR SCHOOL Heptonstall (Calderdale). This is the original C17th grammar school, complete with well used old school furniture and some interesting displays on local history. Also worth seeking out in Heptonstall is the Wesleyan Chapel, an octagonal building dating from 1674 and apparently the oldest continually used Methodist church in the world.

HOLME CHAPEL (Burnley). This unspoilt village is set in the Cliviger Gorge. The Church is of particular interest, being the burial place of several notable people, including General Scarlett, who led the Charge of the Heavy Brigade at Balaclava, his wife Lady O'Hogan, the last resident of Towneley Hall (see under 'Museums') and several notable members of the Towneley family.

HUDDERSFIELD NARROW CANAL (Kirklees). This remarkable feat of engineering, including the famous Standedge Tunnel, is featured in the chapter on 'Transport by Water - The Canals.'

HUDDERSFIELD TOWN HALL Huddersfield. This magnificent building, with its arched windows and decorative roof, has been beautifully restored as the finest Concert Hall in northern England.

HURSTWOOD (Burnley). This tiny village of great charm lies in a sheltered hollow the River Brun. It contains the magnificent Hurtswood Hall, built in 1597, and Tattershall's House, thought to be the oldest building in Hurstwood. You can also see Spenser's Cottage, home of the Elizabethan poet, Edmund Spenser, author of 'The Faerie Queene.' There are several quaint cottages, old farms and great C16th and C17th barns with massive oak timbers, all in remarkable condition.

KEIGHLEY AND WORTH VALLEY RAILWAY The stops on this historic line are Keighley itself, Ingrow, Damens, Oakworth (the one used for the film 'The Railway Children') Haworth and Oxenhope.

KIRKSTALL ABBEY (Leeds). This Norman Abbey, built by the Cistercians in the mid C12th and destroyed by Henry VIII in 1539 under the Dissolution of the Monasteries, remains as Britain's finest early monastic ruin. Oliver Cromwell had a go at it too, doing a certain amount of damage, and it is rumoured to stand above a whole network of secret tunnels, linked not only to churches but also to drinking houses around the area!

LOTHERTON HALL Aberford (Leeds). Strictly speaking east of the area covered by this guide, but well within reach for those visiting Leeds, Lotherton Hall is a largely C18th mansion, which was the home of the Gascoigne family. Their close connections with China have contributed many Oriental works of art to the collections on view in both the house and its beautiful gardens. Ceramics and costume ranging from Edwardian times to the present day are strongly featured in the house. Video presentation and shop.

NOSTELL PRIORY (NT) Wakefield. Another fine house accessible from Leeds, it is not now a priory but an C18th house designed by Paine, with an Adam wing. The rooms still contain the original paintings and Chippendale furniture commissioned, when the house was built, by the owner Sir Rowland Winn. There are fine grounds and the Stable Tea Rooms.

OAKWELL HALL Birstall (Kirklees). This moated manor house dates from 1583, a masterpeice by the Tudor architect John Batt. Its rooms are lined with oak panelling, partly painted, and it is particularly famous for its vast central window. The beautiful formal gardens give way to spreading grounds which now form a Country Park of real distinction. Charlotte Brontë used Oakwell Hall as 'Fieldhead', home of the heroine of her story 'Shirley.' Visitor Centre, workshop and adventure playground.

PIECE HALL Halifax (Calderdale). This breathtaking building, only relatively recently brought to public appreciation by a massive restoration programme, illustrates more dramatically than anything else the size and wealth of the cloth industry in the late C18th. Here, the cottage weavers brought their 'pieces' of cloth to offer them to no less than 315 different merchants. Indeed, weavers travelled from all over Britain and even from the Continent to this spectacular temple of commerce. See also 'Museums.'

ROCHDALE CANAL From Manchester to Sowerby Bridge. This engineering masterpeice by James Brindley is currently being restored. (See 'Transport by Water - The Canals.'

QUEEN STREET MILL Burnley (Burnley). Cloth manufacture eventually stopped being a cottage industry (see the Piece Hall, above) and this is the sort of thing that replaced it - Britain's only steam-powered weaving mill, with its magnificent steam engine 'Peace.' This is where you can experience the sights and sounds of an original C19th Lancashire weaving shed at first hand - living history.

SALTAIRE VILLAGE (Bradford). Sir Titus Salt built this model village between 1852 and 1872 in Italianate style - and then, understandably, gave it a name based on his own. Its interesting buildings include mill, almshouses, church, hospital, institute and school. Visit the 1853 Gallery in Salt's Mill, to see the David Hockney Collection, and the Harmonium Museum (see 'Museums') in Victoria Road.

SHIBDEN HALL Halifax (Calderdale). First built in 1420, this spectacularly beautiful half-timbered building now houses period rooms which illustrate the changes in decorative and furnishing styles over the years. Like Bolling Hall and Oakwell Hall (see above), it too has marvellous collections of oak furniture, some of which has been in the house since Cromwellian times. It is also the home of the West Yorkshire Folk Museum (see under 'Museums').

TEMPLE NEWSAM HOUSE Leeds. This Tudor-Jacobean mansion was built by the Knights Templar and became the property of the D'Arcy family. It was the birthplace of Lord Darnley, ill-fated husband of Mary Queen of Scots. Chippendale furniture is an especial feature of its marvellous contents, which also include paintings, ceramics, silver, sculpture and some fine old wallpapers. The Estate offers excellent woodland walks, a Rare Breeds Centre, Home Farm and gardens which remain spectacular, despite the damage done to them by modern roads.

TOWNELEY HALL (Burnley) See under 'Museums.'

WALKLEY'S CLOG MILL Hebden Bridge (Calderdale). If you want to see and learn about the traditional craft of clog making on a commercial scale, this is your only chance, because Walkley's is the only surviving clog mill in the UK. Here you can see craftsmen at work on the clog soles, clog irons and often beautifully decorated and embossed clog uppers, making everything from serviceable farming clogs to sandal clogs and colourful dancing clogs.

WEAVER'S COTTAGE Rawtenstall (Rossendale). Here you will find a fascinating collection of items connected with the former cottage industry of weaving.

WEAVERS' TRIANGLE (Burnley). In this, one of the best preserved industrial landscapes in Britain, you can see weaving sheds, spinning mills, warehouses, foundries, domestic buildings and a school, all dating from the time when Burnley was cotton capital of the world.

WORSTHORNE (Burnley). A conservation area with a number of listed buildings, including the Church of St John the Evangelist, which is closely associated with the Thursley family, one of whom, the Rev. W. Thursley, was the first incumbent at St John's. His son, Sir John Thursley, gave the land for Queen's Park.

WYCOLLER COUNTRY PARK Colne (Pendle). This is listed here because of its surviving, genuine C19th atmosphere and the fact that it is a working farm, with restoration work in progress. The whole is a conservation area - see also under 'Nature Reserves.'

Lots of interesting towns and villages are to be found in the South Pennines. Many of those on the Lancashire side have been associated with cotton while those on the Yorkshire side are mostly founded on wool. All these cotton wool places differ to a greater or lesser degree, each having its unique characteristics, each making its own special contribution to the composition of the South Pennines as a whole.

ACCRINGTON Sited at the foot of the Pennines to catch the soft water, so vital to the manufacture of cotton, Accrington is where Hargreaves perfected his cotton machinery. At a nearby mill, the first experiments in printing cotton material were carried out. Today textile machines made in Accrington are exported throughout the world. Bricks, manufactured from clay on Whinney Hill are renowned for their longevity. Accrington is fortunately placed, surrounded by hills and with Peel Park to walk in. A gilded weathercock perched on a medieval tower adds a touch of charm and the market hall bursts with produce and Accrington pride.

ADDINGHAM When the Vikings attacked York in 876, the archbishop found refuge in a camp overlooking the River Wharfe close to where Addingham church now stands. The village it serves is near Ilkley and surrounded by hills and moors. Part of the church is over 400 years old, although the building was renovated in the C13th and again between 1947 and 1959. A prized possession is a Late Saxon cross. Samuel Cunliffe Lister, first Baron Masham, is in the family vault there. He devoted his long life to inventing, taking out 150 patents, and invented a wool combing machine that separated long hairs from short ones, bringing prosperity to Bradford and to the Australian wool trade.

BACUP There are a few old houses in Bacup, which is big and modern and to be found in the Irwell Valley, near Rochdale. Near the town centre is St John's, a handsome church built in the 1880s. Nearby, there is another church with an octagonal turret. Stubbylee Park is one of several, all of which are pleasing. Immense, lonely moors ring Bacup with solitude. From the road between Bacup and Burnley can be seen the green mounds of Broadclough Dykes, the remains of an ancient fortification. On the edge of a slope there is a series of embankments more than 400 metres (1,300 ft) long and 16 metres (54 ft) wide along the bottom. These are thought to be an outwork of the battle of Brunanburh, where Saxons under King Athelstan defeated the combined armies of the Danes, the Scots and the Welsh in the C10th.

BARNOLDSWICK 'Barlick'; that's what the locals call this cotton town that is isolated from its church by one mile. The church is surrounded by trees above a lovely glen through which a stream flows to join Early Beck, and is reached along a lane. The chancel is C13th and the east of it, including the tower, is C15th. The altar table is Jacobean, the pews are bobbin-ended, the pulpit a three-decker and the Norman font egg shaped.

BINGLEY Lying on the edge of industrial Yorkshire, Bingley, despite its outer ring of modern housing, is very old indeed. Long before the Romans found it, an ancient tribe built a stone circle there among the heather and placed huge stones at the edge of the moor, supposedly for the purpose of worshipping strange gods. When the Romans returned home, they left a chest at Bingley, containing coins bearing Nero's likeness. The area is rich in fine houses and lovely parks. Myrtle Grove, a fine Georgian house, which John Wesley called a little paradise, is now the Town Hall. Near an C18th footbridge, close to where Harden Beck joins the Aire, stands an old farm, with stone lanterns on its gables and a cross on a stone lintel that tells of when the Knights of St. John once had property there. Bingley has more than its share of old world charm, with flat tombstones in the churchyard separated by narrow ribbons of grass and flowers. A curfew was rung there as recently as 1945. Today a 'pancake bell' is still rung every Shrove Tuesday.

BRIGHOUSE From its commanding place on a steep hillside, Brighouse church looks across the chimneys of this industrial town. Timbers from an old battleship are contained in one of the inns, and one of the houses, Smith House, is where John Wesley preached. Harry Castle Hill offers fine views and Freeman's Wood and Waterclough Valley exude charm.

COLNE The Romans came to Colne and discovered an earthwork on Caster Cliff which they turned into a camp for their legionaries. John Wesley preached here in an overcrowded chapel, despite opposition from a vicar who incited people to attack him. The pillars in the parish church are Norman, the arches they carry are C13th and most of the remainder is Tudor. The porch has a big cube sundial above it. The old grammar school is in the churchyard and some portable stocks are kept there under a roof, their three pairs of holes being mounted on wheels. Beside the old market cross that stands in front of the public library there is a stone shelter. All except one of the names on its walls are war heroes. The odd one out is Wallace Hartley, the Colne bandmaster of the Titanic which sank on its maiden voyage. As the ship was sinking he called on his band to play 'Nearer, my God, to thee'. The band was still playing when the Titanic turned end-on and sank, taking with it 1,500 men and women.

EARBY Once a village and now a busy little cotton town near the Lancashire border, it is best approached from the east. That way it is seen amidst a magnificent panorama of fells, hills and valleys. Its grammar school, now a clinic, being C17th is much older than the parish church, which was built in 1910.

ELLAND The church, standing high in the old part of the town, is mainly C15th, although the chancel arch is probably C13th. It has a sanctus bellcot, a tower with two arches in line with the nave arcade and some lovely woodwork. The font is ancient, as is the glass in the west windows. That in the east windows is modern. Likewise the hymn books are Ancient and Modern. The Fleece Inn in Westgate is thought to be Elizabethan. New Hall, now a farm house, is old and has timbered gables, a rose window, a studded Tudor door and a porch. Elland Hall has little old about it. There is a park above the River Calder and there are some mills in the valley.

HALIFAX A major clothing town, its chief carpet works is probably one of the biggest in the world and it has diversified into engineering, chemicals and machine tools and wire manufacture. The old town is tucked into the deep valley of the River Hebble and the spacious streets and gardens of new Halifax look down on the gaunt chimneys and countless mills of the old. From Beacon, rising steeply on the east side of the river there is a fine view of the town, while from Wainhouse's Tower, a curious C19th stone structure, the views over the moors and the valley are good. The parish church of St John the Baptist is one of only a few really old buildings left in the town. Many fine houses, together with their parks and gardens, now belong to the town, thus giving the people access to over 120 hectares (300 acres) of green spaces. The Public Library and Natural History Museum are housed in Belle View, the home of Sir Francis Crossley, one of Halifax's industrial giants. Bankfield, a grand house to the north of the town, looks like an Italian villa. In it are housed many objets d'art. Away from workaday Halifax, Shibden Hall is the oldest and most gracious of the great houses now owned by the town. It stands in 21 hectares (53 acres) of lovely gardens and grounds and is now an ancient monument. The Town Hall is a Renaissance building designed by Sir Charles Barry, architect of the Houses of Parliament. Halifax has many markets and shopping arcades, including a rather special one. Enclosed by the Old Piece Hall, another of the town's ancient monuments, and in an area of 8,360 square metres (10,000 square yards) is the fruit and vegetable market, which has been held since 1871.

HASLINGDEN With the closure of the mills around St. Stephen's church, the locals decided to move the church, tower, spire and all, stone by stone to its present site 2 miles (3 kms) from the original site. They did most of the work themselves; and left a stone on the old site to tell the tale. A large stone with two holes in it stands near the town's stocks. During the Black Death victims came to this stone to collect food placed there for them. The food was placed in one hole and the payment in another, buyer and seller never meeting.

HAWORTH Standing between lonely moors and the busy valley below it, Haworth is the place to which anyone wishing to understand the Brontës must come. The Parsonage, the Inn and the Church cluster around a melancholy churchyard, as when this famous family lived there. Of the church, the tower is all that remains of the one they knew, the remainder of the building having being built at a later date. The Haworth the Brontës knew was not remote from civilisation. It was a growing industrial town. In 1864, with the Brontës now all gone, the building of the Worth Valley Railway from Keighley to Haworth was begun. In 1881 this little line was taken over by the Midland Railway and continued to operate until 1961.

HEBDEN BRIDGE An old bridge crosses Hebden Water where it joins the River Calder in a hollow of the moors; and around it has grown the pleasant little manufacturing town of Hebden Bridge. 3 miles (5 kms) north-west of the town are the picturesque fir-covered Hardcastle Crags. The area is noted for is fine waterfalls some of which are in lovely Grimsworth valley. Stoodley Hill on which stands Stoodley Pike, is 2 miles (3 kms) south-west of the town. It was erected in 1856 to replace an earlier memorial to Waterloo. Calderdale Leisure Services will tell you all about their excellent feature and more if you pay them a visit.

HEPTONSTALL Surrounded by moorland and perched high on a ridge between the narrow valleys of Hebden Water and the Colden Clough, which join the Calder at Hebden Bridge, Heptonstall is a fascinating mixture of stone houses and crooked streets, too narrow for cars to pass in them. It is said that centuries ago, when Paulinus was persuading King Edwin to accept Christianity, he preached from the ridge on which this historically rich place stands. If you love history wrapped in an atmosphere of old Yorkshire, this is the place for you.

HOLMFIRTH It lies in a deep valley where the Holme and the Ribble meet and steep hillsides climb to heather clad moors dotted with reservoirs. A row of gabled alms-houses with a small spire commemorates the bursting of Bilberry Reservoir in 1852. High on the moors, south of the town, towers the tall Holme Moss TV mast. This town is very popular, through association with 'Last of the Summer Wine'.

HURSTWOOD One of Hurstwood's greatest possessions is Hurstwood Hall, the low, stone, pre-Armada home of the Towneleys. It has delightful little gables and windows, with steps leading down to a gracious porch. It looks across a tiny stream to wooded hills below the moors. Another is a C16th house which for generations was the home of the Spensers. Here, in this house with its oak-raftered ceilings, stone flagged floors and tiny porch, lived Edmund Spenser, one of the outstanding figures of Elizabethan England. It was from this quiet Lancashire hamlet that he went out to become one of, the most precious jewels in Elizabeth's crown.

KEIGHLEY Worsted and woollens, machinery and tools keep Keighley busy. Well sited near the meeting of the Aire and the Worth and edged by moorland, it has strong associations with 4 miles (6½ kms) distant Howarth and the Brontës, who shopped there. It was in Keighley that Charlotte purchased her books and writing paper. From Keighley she took the train to London to launch her immortal 'Jane Eyre'. It was from Keighley Station that Ann entrained to Scarborough, four days before her untimely death. A Keighley man who loved the surrounding lonely moorland is remembered by a huge stone on Haworth Moor, which contains an inscription dedicated to him. Another Keighley man, Timmy Feather, who was baptised by Patrick Bronte in 1825, was the last weaver in England to work at a hand loom. This loom, now in Keighley Museum, has a piece of unfinished cloth on the roller. Cliffe Castle houses the Museum and an Art Gallery. It was given to the town by Sir Bracewell Smith in 1950 and since 1959 has housed the contents of the former Victoria Park Museum, in larger and more modern surroundings. The Castle has rooms devoted to children's games and toys, geology, pre-history, natural history and textiles. St. Andrew's church, on the site of a mediaeval church, was rebuilt in 1805 and again in 1848. A Roman Catholic Church stands on the edge of Keighley. It is shaped like a cross and is built in Norman style. Its walls are of gold tinted stone and it has more than 100 windows.

LEEDS Prehistoric flints have been found within the city boundaries, and there is evidence of Roman occupation. The parish church contains a Saxon cross and the abbey at Kirkstall is medieval. Its first charter was granted in 1626 and it was made a City in 1883. But little of old Leeds remains. It is nevertheless one of the most vital and interesting cities in Britain, rich in cultural and recreational possibilities. See the special feature on Leeds elsewhere in this guide.

LITTLEBOROUGH A Roman Road climbs steeply over Blackstone Edge. The gauge of the wheel ruts is the same as those of the roads of Pompeii and Hadrian's Wall. The road is about 5½ metres (18 ft) wide, including the kerbs, and the camber is seen. On the steep bits a deep groove in the heavy stones along its middle are thought to have been cut or worn by some sort of braking system. Yet otherwise the paving is so little worn that some people believe that, far from being Roman, the road was made by railway people. The first railway to cross the Pennines began at Littleborough and reached its highest point under Summit Ridge in under 1½ miles (2½ kms). The contentious Roman road has a tougher climb from the River Rock to close to where the outcrop of Robin Hood's Bed marks the summit of the Pennine Ridge. Littleborough church was rebuilt last century. Pike House is C17th and C16th Stubbley Old Hall is one of the oldest houses in this part of the country. Nearby Hollingworth Lake is one of many man-made lakes in the South Pennines.

LOTHERSDALE Usually quarries provide only stone but Raygill quarry, near Lothersdale provided the bones of a mammoth. Usually flightpaths are followed by aircraft; but Lothersdale, in its deep valley in the heart of the moors, is on a flightpath used by witches en route to Pendle. Ledges protruding from some of the cottage chimneys were placed there deliberately so that any witch suffering from flight fatigue might rest there to eat food provided by the residents. The village provided a safe refuge for Quakers during the reign of Charles II, and in the village Meeting House there is a gallery which has hatches for people to look through. The village Church is sited on a hillside high above it and has magnificent views of the surrounding moors. At a higher level and hidden in trees is Stonegappe, which Charlotte Brontë called Gateshead in 'Jane Eyre'.

MELTHAM Two Iron Age settlements have been discovered at this exposed hilly place. The church dates from 1651 but little except a date-stone remains of the original. It was extensively rebuilt between 1782 and 1786 and its west tower was added in 1835.

MILNROW There is a church at each end of this small mill town. One was built by George Street, who designed London's Law Courts. Inside the other, the font has eight delightful scenes cut into it. One depicts Noah and his family leaving the ark with two elephants and a giraffe and the others are in similar vein.

OLDHAM In 1630 linen was introduced into Oldham. At the end of the next century cotton was king and this was the way of it. Richard Arkwright had introduced a number of technical improvements in the manufacture of cotton yarn and played an important part in the change from manual power to mechanical power. He re-introduced spinning by rollers and in 1769 patented a water- driven spinning frame. In 1775, with the patenting of his carding machine, he successfully mechanised the whole of cotton spinning. James Watt invented a separate condenser for his steam engine that reduced the cost of steam power by 75%. Coal was found nearby and the air was found to be sufficiently damp to prevent the cotton threads snapping. By the beginning of the C19th the cotton trade was in full swing and Oldham quickly developed the reputation as the number one cotton-spinning town in the world, having the largest textile engineering works and one of the biggest outputs of cotton velvet. The number of mills continued to grow and eventually numbered about 250, with 18 million spindles. So through hard work, cotton and coal, Oldham became the epitome of the Industrial Revolution. Oldham has art as well as industry. Its Art Gallery is famous, and like its cotton and machines, reproductions of its pictures have gone all over the world. Yet Oldham and its surroundings are not all cotton and art. Diversification has taken place with organisations like Pennine Moonraker of Saddleworth and Clough Bottom Nurseries being proud to be part of the area's success, a view heartily endorsed by Thameside Metropolitan Borough Council. Annually on the last Saturday in August, Oldham shuts shop and goes on holiday, for it is then that the famous Wakes begin.

OTLEY Otley Chevin is a great hill ridge which offers panoramic all-round views; and Otley lies beneath it. Sited on the edge of industrial Yorkshire, it makes worsted and leather and printing machines. For a thousand years dales folk have come to sell their wool in this little town, which still has an ancient seven-arched bridge, a court house dated 1875, several old houses and inns and a maypole.

PADIHAM A colliery town surrounded by parks - that's Padiham. One, the Pease Memorial Park, made in memory of its heroes, has a museum, a rose garden, a sunken pool and a view of distant hills. It has three Elizabethan houses, Gawthorpe, which has a square tower in the middle and perhaps the remains of a keep, High Whitaker, with its secret rooms, where the priest, Thomas Whitaker is said to have lived until he was captured there and killed at Lancaster, and Huntroyde, where Gendre Starkie lived about a century ago.

RAWTENSTALL The houses and mills of Rawtenstall are tucked into deep, twisting valleys hemmed in by the Rossendale Fells. Whitaker Park, which is draped over a steep hill, contains an art gallery that is linked with one of the best museums in the North. Rawtenstall is in the middle of Lancashire's shoe and slipper world. The Cenotaph and Garden of Remembrance are in the middle of the town. It has several modern churches but the finest in the neighbourhood is St. John's at Crawshawbooth, which is on a wooded slope and has a stream flowing past the churchyard.

SHIPLEY Once a village in a green valley, Shipley is now a centre of the worsted trade and has factories and iron foundries. Its modern church, built in C15th style, looks from its high site across the River Aire to the moors. The town is proud of its reconstructed town centre which has a prominent clock tower in the middle of it.

SILSDEN Augustus Spencer, Principal of the Royal College of Art from 1900 to 1920, was born in this workaday place with its canal, its worsted mills and its nail factories. There is a memorial to him in the C18th church.

SLAITHWAITE This quiet little village is tucked into a deep valley where the River Colne, a railway and a canal are side by side; and where there are two viaducts. Its church dates from 1790 but there has been one there since 1590. On the high hills rising far above the mills are the huge masts of the Moorside Edge Broadcasting Station.

SOWERBY BRIDGE This busy little town, its walls blackened by smoke from mills and manufacturing works, is in the narrow Calder valley. In 1770 John Foster, a farmer's son who became a preacher and essayist, was born there. There are several C17th houses nearby.

WYCOLLER This remote and beautiful place, lying in a hollow at the foot of Trawden Forest, between windy moors, is divided by a stream that tumbles and splashes under seven bridges, one of which is a double-arched C13th gem. Another, so-called Druid bridge, is simply three huge stones supported by a boulder, 4½ metres (15 ft) long and 60 centimetres (2 ft) wide, used by hand-loom weavers. On dark nights those crossing it felt for the hollow at the end, then crept over, sliding one foot after the other along a depression worn through time. Another is a single monolith with its great weight supported by boulders on either bank. These bridges enhance the great charm of this sturdy, stone house village which has seen little change for 300 years. There is no church and nearby Wycoller Hall, once the home of the famous Hartley and Cunliffe families is ruinous, its lavish, fortnight-long Christmas festivities long since gone. It was Charlotte Brontë who came to Wycoller Hall from Haworth Vicarage, over the moors, to gaze, entranced, at this empty hall; and who in her imagination later transformed it into Fearndean Manor to which Jane Eyre fled on learning Rochester's secret, making it immortal. Here, truly, is a place not to be missed. For here, as with so many other places in the South Pennines, the ordinary has become extra-ordinary thanks to the endeavours of some very extra-ordinary South Pennine people, aided and abetted by some extra-ordinary South Pennines countryside.

HOTELS

FARMHOUSE ACCOMMODATION

CARAVAN & CAMPING SITES

CRAFTS & CRAFTSMEN

SHOPPING

EATING OUT

GARDEN CENTRES

PLACES TO VISIT & THINGS TO DO